HOPE STREET

Pamela Young is a retired social worker. She grew up in north-west England and still lives there with her husband Simon. Pamela has three granddaughters and spends a lot of time with her family. In her spare time she enjoys visiting sacred places and going on spiritual pilgrimages. She also likes walking, reading and meditating.

Pamela Young
HOPE STREET

CORONET

First published in Great Britain in 2011 by Coronet
An imprint of Hodder & Stoughton
An Hachette UK company

First published in paperback in 2012

1

A CIP catalogue record for this title is available from the British Library

ISBN 978 1 444 71425 8

Typeset in Sabon MT by Palimpsest Book Production Limited,
Falkirk, Stirlingshire

Printed and bound by Clays Ltd, St Ives plc

Hodder & Stoughton policy is to use papers that are natural, renewable
and recyclable products and made from wood grown in sustainable forests.
The logging and manufacturing processes are expected to conform to the
environmental regulations of the country of origin.

Hodder & Stoughton Ltd
338 Euston Road
London NW1 3BH
www.hodder.co.uk

Foreword

It was a glorious summer's day in 2006 when I first met Pamela Young. She and her husband, Simon were staying with a great friend of mine, and we met in the magnificent setting of Mount Usher Gardens, in County Wicklow.

The minute I met her I felt I'd known her all my life. There was that moment of 'recognition' that she writes about, when 'Soul Family' connects. And I'm absolutely sure we've known each other in many lifetimes. There was a lot of laughter that day and I listened fascinated as she told me of her background and 'The Work' she had come back to do in this lifetime.

We became great friends and in January 2008 she came to spend a week with me to work on the manuscript of this amazing book. It is such a rich tapestry. Reading it, I felt I knew her wonderful mother, Evelyn who *lived* her philosophy of service, helping family, friends and anyone who needed her in a most truly non-judgemental way. The story of the family's membership of the Horwich Spiritualist Church and the home circle which Evelyn formed in Hope Street, where they lived, is utterly absorbing. A circle of seven dedicated sitters, all hailed from very ordinary backgrounds but had something unique and special to offer. This was long before Mind, Body and Spirit workshops.

The account of the social history of the era, the life and times, joys and hardships of ordinary people that she writes about will touch a chord with so many readers as will the beautiful messages that Pam has been given to share with the world. Pam is very aware that her gifts have been given by Spirit. There is nothing of the ego in her. She was very hesitant about writing her story but how wonderful that she has because what has been revealed to her is truly life changing. Her description of the Soul Mothers, singing young souls to their birth is utterly moving. Her descriptions of life when we have passed over are joyful.

Today many write books of doom and gloom, of terrible futures. Many write of a wrathful, vengeful God, and contribute to the misery and fear that lowers the vibration of our world. In this book the message to us who are enfolded in 'the Great Forgetting' is a call to remember whom we *really* are, radiant beings filled with Divine DNA.

When you read Hope Street, you are uplifted, exhilarated, excited at the profound truths that shine through. This radiant book will bring great comfort, healing and hope to all who are blessed by reading it.

I am greatly honoured to write this foreword and so blessed by Pam's loving friendship.

Introduction
by Patricia Scanlan

This book started to come to me five years ago in a series of dreams and visions, but its true beginnings stem from the early 1860s, when my great-grandmother was born in South Africa and my great-grandfather was born in east Manchester. Coming from two very different continents, cultures and life experiences, these adventurous souls were nevertheless destined to meet. Their union was to start a family that, after two generations of strong, gifted women, would result in the arrival of my mother Evelyn, a trance medium who could communicate with the Spirit world in a remarkable way, channelling its message here on the material plane.

I believe this book was written long before I was born, but I also believe it was written in the Spirit world with the agreement of my Spirit and angel guides. (I will explain later what I mean by my Spirit and angel guides.) It was my job to bring it into being here with help from my Spirit family, both on this earth and in the world unseen. This may sound like a grand claim from a very ordinary grandmother but I am certain this is true.

What's more I believe that everyone here on earth has a unique mission to help fulfil a common goal – that is, to bring light into this world. This may take the form of little acts of kindness that we perform in our everyday lives or it may be acted out on a more global scale – for example, a president or a princess pursuing their amazing, inspirational and flawed lives in the public domain, touching the hearts of millions and uniting them in love, grief and shared humanity. The rest of us may make comparisons and see our individual contribution as very small, but light does not discriminate. One smile can start a reverberation around the planet and have far-reaching consequences, amazing but yet unseen by us. Every time we touch another's heart we heal the world a little, and our respondent is equally important in this process. However insignificant we feel, or however bad or good we perceive ourselves to be, we can be sure that each one of us has a huge effect upon the collective consciousness through our actions. We are all spiritual pilgrims on an evolutionary journey of awakening.

There is a saying: 'We are not human beings having a spiritual experience; we are spiritual beings having a human experience.' If we all try to tell our individual and unique stories, this may help us become aware of a unifying principle – a power greater than ourselves – guiding and leading us. As signs of this unifying principle, we may find that we have experienced little miracles along the way, synchronicities when that special someone or special something has come along at just the right time to help us. We may have had mystical experiences, dreams or strong intuitions that have led us onto the right path.

But more often than not we learn through adversity. During those times of darkness we may finally surrender ourselves and call for help to a higher power. We may often feel it is external to ourselves, but it is actually vibrantly alive within every one of us.

This is my story, the story of my awakening to who and what I am, deep beyond my transient personality on the temporal plane. Inevitably, my recollections from personal experiences and things learned from relatives may be flawed. If I have made mistakes and upset people, I ask them to forgive me. I write with a good heart with the intention of sharing the message of Spirit, which cannot be told without touching on the lives of others in my family, past and present.

I have come to realise that Spirit has a unifying principle, that it has been working through our family according to a plan. Over four generations, it has been working to help bring a message to the world.

A higher power has led me to write *Hope Street* and I follow its direction with total trust and faith. I have found it hard to expose myself in the course of writing this book and there have been times when I have been afraid and wished I'd never started. But as you will see in the pages that follow I was compelled to do this; it was never a matter of choice. I have been guided throughout my life with love and understanding by my family, who have blessed me with the greatest joys and the greatest challenges, but more than anything I have been guided by the love of Spirit.

When I started to write five years ago, I had no idea where it would go or why I was doing it; I just knew I had to do it. If I say it came out as automatic writing that might give the wrong impression. But like automatic writing, it was very swift, and I didn't have to 'think' about the words. They seemed to come from a place beyond my normal thinking mind, but it didn't feel like it was coming from outside of myself or from an external Spirit. It was almost as if it had always been in me, programmed, just waiting for me to download it when the time was right. It was as though I had been born with this information and I had called upon it only now because I was ready.

Five years on and without much effort on my part I am being published. I was led to people and places, which then led me to more people and places. Significantly, I was given a book about the esoteric knowledge of the world and upon reading its pages I instinctively felt that I 'knew' the author, even though I had never met him. He was a kindred spirit and already I felt love for him. Within days of receiving his book and having read the introduction about twenty times, I wrote to him in the same almost unconscious way I wrote the original manuscript for my book. It was compelling and swift, and without my thought and ego getting in the way I wrote the following:

Dear Mark,

I am a retired soul worker. I am an ordinary woman, but with an extraordinary story to tell. I was born into a family who communed with Spirit day and night. My mother was a trance medium, and all my life has been dedicated to what we called The Work and to the Divine Imagination [. . .]

I am writing to you on the directions of Spirit. These are special times when we are in the midst of a huge transformation. Humanity is on the cusp of great changes in consciousness [. . .]

I leave it to Spirit to move things in the way they wish, but I am in no doubt that we shall meet very soon and recognise our strong bonds and soul mission.

In love and light,
Pamela

Later I looked again at the copy on the computer and cringed to see that I had described myself as a 'retired soul worker' instead of a 'retired social worker'! Well, I thought, that will surely go straight in the nutter's bin. But not only did he write back, but this man, a respected author, turned out to be a publisher himself in a well-known publishing house. He asked to see what I had written and became intrigued by my family history, especially the stories about my mother Evelyn and her lifelong commitment to working with Spirit. In one of those strange twists of fate that seem to follow me, he offered to publish my manuscript, which has become the book you are now holding.

In the 1950s my family had been sworn to secrecy about the sittings where the Spirits would come through my mother and tell us things, but after fifty-five years of keeping these secrets I suddenly felt compelled to write about Mam's Spiritual calling. Five years ago, in the spring of 2005, I started to have a kind of awakening, a renewed and vibrant feeling about Spirit. Suddenly I felt compelled to share the things our family had been told. This information had been kept secret, not because we thought it might get us into trouble, but because the content of these startling revelations was unheard of at the time. We were a working-class family in the north of England. Nobody would have believed us.

These revelations, which the Spirit friends called 'The Work', were channeled through my mam when she was in trance. In those days it wasn't called channeling – the process was known as 'going through' or 'going under'. Mediumship was not uncommon in the 1940s and '50s and the Spiritualist Church was well-established. As a family we were members of the Horwich Spiritualist Church and we had a home circle, which was not unusual among the congregations of the Church. Hope Street, where we lived, was where my mam formed a circle of seven dedicated sitters. These sitters gave much of their lives in service to Spirit, but they received much more in return.

Hope Street, Horwich, is where I was born in 1948 and had my first experiences of Spirit. I was too young to be present at the early circles but Mam and Dad and the sitters have retold these wonderful memories so many times that sometimes I find it hard to be sure whether I was there or not.

In this book I have written not only about my family history, our trials and our tribulations, and our remarkable and enduring relationship with Spirit, but I have also tried to capture the feeling of the times. Just after the Second World War there was peace and a new hope. Socialism was part of a new consciousness that gave birth to the National Health Service, the nationalisation of the railways and other initiatives that we take for granted today. There was optimism and jobs for all, giving people a purpose and the sense of having a valued place in society. A feeling of well-being swept the nation as the first generation of baby boomers were born. They in their turn would enlighten the 1960s with their revolutionary concepts of flower power and free love.

As well as attempting to evoke the general feeling of the times as I grew up, I have also written about the remarkable pioneering history of Horwich, which I believed played such a large role in our life as a family and as a community. Similarly I have recorded the history of modern Spiritualism, as this movement played an essential part in my upbringing.

Connections old and new have helped me to see things from a fresh perspective, and in telling my story I have realised that the answer to the great mystery can only be found inside ourselves, as we journey along our unique and winding path. But as Spiritualism teaches, we are not alone as we trudge along the road of our destiny. We are constantly guided not only by the world of Spirit, which is eternal, but also by our guides here on earth. I like to call these people earth-angels and we are attracted to them by the synchronicity of light.

I should be clear that it has not all been inspiration and Spiritual contentment in my life; there have been times when I have had to travel through darkness. But now, sixteen years after my mother's death, I am able to present this book as part of that journey. This is my story, my path to under-standing myself, and my awakening to something eternal and full of love. I hope you find something in its pages to inspire you.

Part One

A Spiritualist Childhood

I was born at home in the early hours of 29 April 1948, after a five-hour Spirit sitting in our three-up, two-down council house in Horwich. My mother's labour pains began coming immediately after the sitting ended. Our family lived on Hope Street, a road that runs from the centre of town on one side to the beautiful countryside of Rivington at the other. Working-class through and through, Horwich is an industrial town of around 20,000 people, which sits between Bolton and Chorley in the West Pennines. It nestles in the shadow of Rivington Pike, a large, breast-shaped hill offering views over Lancashire, Cheshire and Wales, with Blackpool Tower clear on the horizon.

Horwich was then, and still remains in my heart today, the place where I belong. The young girl who took her first steps on its cobbled lanes and the woman I am now have both been shaped by its beautiful landscape, its people, its history and its industry.

The sense of place was powerful, but so too were the forces of Spirit. Spirit was our family's natural element, and from a baby I was brought up living and breathing the two worlds. I took our Spirit life for granted as a young child. I had nothing else to compare it to so it seemed totally normal to me.

And for the most part my life was very normal

for a young northern girl of the time. Some of my earliest memories are of waiting for my dad to come home for his dinner – which is what we call lunch in our part of the world – from his job at the loco works. I remember vividly sitting on his knee and feeling both fascinated and repulsed at seeing Dad's whole scalp covered with black coal specks, glistening through his thinning fair hair.

Dad was a good-looking man with a wide smile. As he spent most of his week covered in coal dust it was very important to him that his weekend going-out clothes were perfect. On a Friday night, Mam would have a beautifully ironed shirt waiting for him, hung on the old clothes rack suspended from the ceiling on a pulley system. Dad would polish his shoes to a shine and would look immaculate but for his hands, which were always stained black from the coal no matter how many times he washed them.

These memories of my dad are so sharp and full of longing that even today I can feel the love and expectation I used to experience waiting for him to walk through that door. We would have our main meal, which we called tea, at about six o'clock, usually a stew or potato hash. But Dad's midday meal would always be something like egg and bacon, or a boiled egg or some butties, washed down with a cup of strong, steaming tea. The wireless would be on and I can still hear the distinctive voice on the BBC Home Service saying,

'*And now the shipping forecast . . . Viking, North Utsire . . . Six to gale force eight . . . Forties, Cromarty . . . Dogger, Fisher, German Bight . . . mainly fair . . . Severe gale eight . . . rising slowly.*'

Our house was one of hundreds built in the area in the 1930s. It was a real 'step up' for families who had been brought up – like my mother and grandmother – with gas lighting, a tin bath, an outside lav and a pot under the bed. These new council houses had ground floors made of local red brick, with cream pebbledash on the upper floors. They were all identical, but compared to the cottages built back-to-back for the mill workers a generation earlier, they were palaces.

The smartest room in our house, the front room, had a dresser and a settee with two chairs facing the marble fireplace. It was rarely used when I was a child apart from when special visitors came, so it was always kept neat and tidy for this purpose. We tended to give it a wide berth – we knew better than to make a mess of 'Mam's front room'.

Instead, the kitchen was the heart of our family home. We would nearly always enter the house by the back door, even though this meant walking round the side. There was a small cooker next to the sink and a draining board under the window where there was always a vase of freshly cut flowers in spring and summer. There was also a cupboard and a small kitchen table and chairs on an oilcloth flooring. Mam always ensured her kitchen was scrupulously clean so we always tried to help her keep it that way, though sometimes Dad's playful nature got the better of his common sense. I remember one day we received something in the post that was packed in a box full of sawdust. Before we knew it, Dad had scattered the sawdust all over the kitchen floor, turned the table upside down so that it became our boat, and with our imaginary oars we were soon crossing the high seas, singing and avoiding the pirates and crocodiles on our way to Fiji. I can still remember my mam's face when she got back from the shops and saw the state of her kitchen.

In the corner of the kitchen was the radiogram, which provided us with the world news, the hit parade and much of our family's entertainment. It was a small piece of furniture in gleaming polished wood, housing a wireless, a record player and inbuilt speakers. There was also an open fire where we would make toast with a toasting fork. I can still recall the butter from the toast running down my chin as I listened to the radio. We listened to the wireless all the time because music was a big feature in our house, and we often had singalong nights.

Years after the war, we still had the blackout blinds from the air raids at the kitchen window, as we couldn't afford to replace them with proper curtains. But back in the days when we used to hold the sittings in the kitchen, I think that these old blinds were probably useful for the sessions held during the summer months when we needed to create the right low-lit atmosphere for Spirit to come through. A red bulb would be placed in the ceiling rose, its soft glow casting the perfect light for Mam to go into her trance and let the Spirits speak through her. There was never a time when Spirit was not in our lives. It infused everything.

I can clearly recall evenings spent sitting in the kitchen eating my supper of pobs – pieces of bread with warm milk and sugar sprinkled over. After patiently waiting for me to finish, Dad would carry me in his arms through to the lounge where I would kiss my mother and say goodnight not just to her but to the Spirit friends she channeled. Different Spirits would say pleasant things to me in different voices. I don't remember the words, just the warm feelings their voices gave me. Dad would then carry me upstairs and tuck me up, but ten minutes later my brother and I would sneak out of bed and sit at the top of the stairs with our faces pressed against the banister, listening intently to the goings-on downstairs and waiting for more Spirit friends to talk through my mam, amazed at the different voices that came through her. It seemed as if our home was like a railway junction spanning heaven and earth.

Upstairs there was a bathroom and three bedrooms: two double rooms and a tiny boxroom. The landing was so narrow you could hardly turn around in it. Mam and Dad had the front bedroom and my older brother Thomas and I shared a bed in the back room until he was five, when he moved into the boxroom. Thomas was three years older than me, a bonny child with blonde curly hair, and he used to patiently teach me all manner of interesting things. I can clearly recall the thrill I felt when he taught me to tie my shoelaces and to tell the time. Generous to a fault, he would always share his sweets with me. He was a wonderful older brother.

All the council houses in Horwich built in the thirties came with substantial gardens, and ours was long and secluded thanks to a thick privet hedge. The hedge sloped downwards as it neared the house, so a chat with the next-door neighbour was a common occurrence. After the hardships of their childhoods and six years of war, Mam and Dad loved tending their garden. Here Mam grew flowers, mainly pansies and sweet william, in remembrance of her late father. He had died when she was only four but she had a strong relationship with him in Spirit. She also planted a lovely purple rhododendron, a plant that grows well in these parts, and they had a beautiful pink climbing rose on a trellis overhanging the back door, which had the most delicious scent.

The back garden was big enough for my dad to have a vegetable plot, and he provided the family with potatoes, carrots and runner beans.

The front garden was small but still had pansies, a privet hedge and a gate, which Dad would lean on and watch the world go by. Every passer-by would stop for a chat; they all knew each other in our street. In fact most of the men worked together at the loco works where my dad and his father before him were engineers. These days people just want to shut their front doors and keep the world out, but back then folk lived on their doorsteps, talking to each other and keeping an eye on the comings and goings. Now it would be considered nosiness but back then it was just the way we lived. All the houses faced each other, so everyone knew what was going on, especially on a Friday and Saturday when the men would return from the pub singing.

As you came in through our back door there was a little coal hole just inside the kitchen. The coal men used to arrive on an open-sided coal lorry tightly packed with their sacks of shiny fuel. They would lean backwards and, with a quick jolt, hitch the coal onto their backs, holding the corners of the sack tightly with their gloved hands. As they came around to empty their heavy loads into our black hole, all I noticed were the whites of their eyes and teeth smiling out of their blackened faces.

We also had regular visits from the rag and bone man, trotting down Hope Street on his horse and cart. He would shout something that didn't sound like 'rag and bone' at all, but there was no mistaking his loud request. You would have to be quick to get out to him before he trotted on past. I remember being very excited one day when we got a goldfish, our first pet, in exchange for our unwanted stuff, only to find it dead the next morning.

The folks who lived on Hope Street were the salt of the earth and would do anything to help each other. I remember a lovely woman who lived two doors away called Mrs Gerard. She was as broad as she was tall, with the biggest bust I had ever seen. She was the one everyone would go to in an emergency. I still remember, after I fell over in the street one day, being swept up into her arms and enfolded in her warm, comforting and ample bosom until I stopped crying. Mam also told me about one day in our kitchen when I was dozing on Grandma's knee as she was using the treadle sewing machine. When the sewing machine started I woke with a jolt and banged my head on the chair. I cried so hard that I held my breath and then fainted. Mam ran upstairs to get my dad who was in bed, being on nights at that time. He jumped up and ran up the street in his underpants to fetch Mrs Gerard. She came rushing in and cuddled me until I recovered.

I was about six when Mrs Gerard died and I remember sitting on the side of the sink by the kitchen window, looking up into the sky to watch for her going to heaven. After about two hours when there was still no sign of her, my dad lifted me down, gently explaining that she was probably already there.

I loved playing on the floor in our warm little kitchen, listening to the radio or to Mam and Dad chatting. My parents were great talkers. Both socialists and trade unionists, they were forever discussing the state of the world. Dad also liked to tell us stories about the goings-on at work and all the tricks they played on each other. There was one workmate who used to repair his own shoes by sticking rubber soles onto the bottoms. But he was not up to much when it came to making a good finish and often great lumps of rubber would stick out round the edge where he hadn't bothered to trim them off. Now the locomotive works was a very noisy place, full of hammering and crashing of machinery, so one day, one of his mates got him talking while someone else sneaked up behind him and nailed the rubber edges of his shoes to the floor – the workshop was so noisy that one or two extra bangs was not going to be noticed. The poor man had no idea what was going on until he went to walk away, only to find that he was rooted to the spot. He ended up sprawled on the floor, much to everybody's amusement.

Another tale Dad loved to tell was of a workmate who complained that his missus never welcomed him home at noon with a cooked meal. Horrified, his workmates sent him home to put her in her place and demand that she make him a hot dinner the next day. He arrived at work the following morning after laying down the law. He was triumphant: she had promised there would be something in the oven for him that day. Later, when he got home, there was a note on the table saying, 'Your dinner's in the oven.' Upon opening the oven door he found a dish with two bob in it and another note saying, 'Go to chippy'!

Dad was always coming back with funny stories about his friends from work. The works outings, for example, were called 'picnics', although there was never a picnic as such, just a day out. Rather than pay for the trip at the time and all at once, the workers would chip in a couple of bob a week to the 'picnic fund' so that it would all be paid for when the time came. Come the great day, all the men would pile into a charabanc and set off. The routine was always the same. On the way they would stop off at a pub just outside Blackpool and have their dinner washed down with plenty of beer. Once in Blackpool they would split up into groups and do much the same as we would today, walking up and down the prom, stopping at pubs on the way, going into the penny arcades and filling up on fish and chips. At the end of the day they would all climb back into the 'chara,' and sing their hearts out all the way home with songs like 'Goodnight Irene', Mairzy Doats' and 'You Always Hurt the One You Love'.

On two occasions that I know of the picnic went badly wrong. On the first of these, the entire works were assembled at the pick-up point at ten o'clock in the morning waiting for the chara ... and waiting ... and waiting. After an hour, someone was sent to the chara office to find out what was going on. The man returned to announce that nothing had been booked, and the money collector, Billy, was nowhere to be found. The men split up and scoured Horwich looking for Billy to get the situation sorted. Eventually they found him wandering vaguely round muttering, 'Who am I? Where am I?' He claimed that he'd been attacked, hit over the head, robbed of all the money and had lost his memory to boot. Not satisfied with this tale, the workers persuaded Billy that it would be in his interests to get his memory back pretty quickly. It turned out that he had hit himself over the head with a frying pan, having squandered all their money on a widow woman. From that day on, Dad said, he was know as 'Frying Pan Billy'.

Another time they discovered the picnic was cancelled a few days before they were due to go. The money collector came into work one day and announced that his house had been broken into, and – surprise, surprise – all the picnic money had been stolen. Nothing else had been taken, only the picnic fund. When the break-in was investigated, it turned out that the 'thief' had broken in by smashing a window from the *inside*, so all the broken glass was in the garden. Once he was exposed, the picnic collector admitted that he had spent all the money on boozing. My dad used to call them daft buggers, for thinking they could get away with it, but I often used to wonder who the real daft buggers were – those who took the money or those who kept giving it to them.

Everyone at the works seemed to have a nick-name and there was so much larking about I wonder that they ever got any work done at all.

It must have been at one of those midday dinners with my dad that I experienced real fear for the first time. I remember quite clearly my dad walking in one dinnertime and saying there was going be another war. My parents were very sombre that day and I was frightened, although I didn't know what a war was. I found out later that he had been talking about the Suez Canal crisis.

My dad read widely and would have had plenty of opinions about this. My parents were very aware of what was going on in the outside world, and had strong beliefs and values that were instilled in us at every opportunity. They were staunch believers in the doctrine, 'From each according to their abilities, to each according to their need,' and it was drilled into us from an early age to be truly grateful for all our blessings. We were also taught to listen and treat people with respect even if we didn't agree with their views. My parents believed that discernment and understanding could come only from 'walking a mile in the other man's shoes'. We were taught to discuss, never argue, and – in a very simple, plain-speaking fashion – to philosophise and try to gain a higher perspective on life.

When it started, Spiritualism was considered as modern and progressive as socialism, and my parents were young firebrands at the forefront of both movements. They integrated and acted from their spiritual and political convictions, each serving the notion of the brotherhood of man.

For example, one simple but powerful concept that was constantly reinforced in our household was the idea that 'thought is a living thing.' This may not be considered revolutionary now, when there are countless books written on the Law of Attraction and Cosmic Ordering, but in the 1950s it was exceptional. My Mam claims my first words were 'Buddy 'ell', when I saw her darning my dad's black socks with red wool, but I suspect my first words were actually, 'Fought is a liffing fing.'

In those days what is now known as the extended family was very important too. Everyone lived just round the corner, and most days would find us gathered in the kitchen by the fire; me, Mam, Dad, my brother, and my beloved cousin. Angela lived around the corner with my maternal grandma – 'Little Grandma' I called her – and Grandma's youngest daughter, Joan. Angela was a very powerful presence in my life in those early years and indeed even today. She was more like an older sister than a cousin and her name suited her because she had both the looks and disposition of an angel. Nine years older than me and six years older than my brother, she was a great teacher who held us spellbound with stories of adventure and magic. Sometimes she took us to the woods and a secret place she called 'Raspberry Valley' and, when we got there, she would tell us magical stories about fairies and goblins. Angela and my brother Thomas both had lovely, happy natures and were great fun. They were popular, confident and clever, and both got on well at school.

In common with many of my generation we had an enormous freedom as children to just run off and play by ourselves, totally unsupervised, returning home only for meals. Of course there were hardly any cars around in those days so us kids played out in the street all the time – occasionally getting into scraps. Although I might have appeared to be a bit soft and a mammy's girl – 'mard' as they say up here – I could also be a proper madam when riled. My brother said that I looked like a wild warrior woman when I got going. On one occasion I was in the street when a neighbour's son gave me a piece of chewing gum. I was thrilled and started happily chewing away – at which point he said: 'Tricked you – it's to make you go!' Well, all I can remember is spitting the laxative out, lunging towards the boy, heaving him over his privet hedge, then running for home. I streaked through our kitchen into the front room and hid breathless behind the couch. Had I got away with it?

A moment later there was a very loud knock at the back door and the sounds of a crying boy being comforted by his mother. My mam opened the door, and bellowed the word I had been dreading: 'PAMELA!' I crept into the kitchen and cowered in front of the two mothers and the snotty-nosed kid. I was half the size of this boy, who was two years older than me. The women looked at me and then looked at him and looked back at me again, and shook their heads in disbelief. As Mam closed the door she looked at me again and for a moment I saw just the slightest flicker of doubt in her eyes . . . and then the nod of her head told me I had got away with it.

As children we were always included in all aspects of family life whether it was happy, sad, good or bad news. Ours was a family with a history of great comings and goings, not just in this world but the next one too. And there was certainly no shortage of characters in our family dramas. Both the grandmothers were frequent visitors. Grandma Heath, my dad's mother, was a slightly formidable woman, with an imposing, upright appearance, who arrived dressed very smartly in belted rain-coats with padded shoulders. She was tall with white permed hair and a handsome face, large eyes and a wide mouth that my dad had inherited. She always struck me as quite stern and a bit 'better' than us – in sharp contrast to my lovely 'Little Grandma', Grandma Smart, Mam's mother.

Little Grandma was softly spoken and didn't have as broad an accent as other Horwichers, a hangover from the little bit of private education her parents had been able to afford, I think. A petite woman, she was probably only about five feet tall, with lovely warm, twinkly brown eyes and short, curly dark hair. She always looked beautiful to me. Like Mam, she had shapely legs and wore straight skirts below the knee and little heels that showed them off to their best advantage. Looking after their appearance was very important to the women in my family and they did the best they could with the little money they had.

My mam took after her dad with her hazel eyes, unlike her other siblings who inherited the dark looks of their mother and grandmother. Mam, a very slender woman, always wished she was a bit more rounded, though I always thought she looked elegant. I remember her rummaging through the tables of jumble at the second-hand clothes shop on the lane looking for bargains. I've no doubt Grandma Smart was there rummaging too as our family certainly had no money for new clothes.

Other regular visitors included Auntie Alice, Mam's cousin. They had been at school together and had even lived together after Mam left home.

Then there was our neighbour Auntie Doris, who was always popping round for a natter and cuppa. She wasn't a real auntie but it would have been considered rude for kids to call her by her first name without the 'Auntie' prefix.

The other important figure in our extended family was my dad's brother, Uncle Fred. Our house on Hope Street is where he had lived with his mam, dad and my dad Arthur before the war. Unlike Dad who, as an engineer, was in a reserved occupation, Fred had joined up and was in the army catering corps. On his return he brought his sweetheart, Auntie Bella, with him, and they did a bit of their courting at the house on Hope Street before they married. Like my dad, Uncle Fred was friendly and full of fun and, also like Dad, he was a very good-looking, fair-haired man with a ready smile, slightly taller and thinner than my dad (who, although slim, was of a stockier build). They were both Socialists, but Uncle Fred was far more left-wing, confident in his opinions and capable of being very assertive. As kids we adored him. He had two mantras that he would trot out time and again: 'If you can't say anything good about a person, don't say anything,' and, 'They're doing their best.' He truly believed in the brotherhood of man like the rest of our family and as a result of these various influences I was raised with a unique complementary blend of politics and Spiritualism informing my upbringing.

I was extremely close to my mother but my cosy life at home with her couldn't last forever and when the time came for me to start school it was a dreadful wrench. A serious child and a late developer, I was incredibly clingy with Mam and must have been a real monster at times, insisting on my special chair in the mornings and always having to be persuaded to go to school. I could be very tricky and until the age of eight would hardly eat at all, with the consequence that I was a very skinny little girl. I was always being told that children in Africa would be so grateful for my food and I couldn't understand why we couldn't just send it to them. When Mam got really anxious about me I was given something called malt and slippery elm to help me put on weight (I am sure it has a forty-year delay before really taking effect).

I disliked school with a passion and was always trying to escape back home. I hated any separation from my mother. Separation and feelings of loss are things I have struggled with and felt deeply throughout my life – Mam said it was because I found it hard to adjust when I returned this lifetime. Although I wanted to do well at school, I just couldn't seem to grasp things. It was a time of humiliation and embarrassment. I hated saying goodbye to Mam and after she had dropped me off in the morning she would often have to come back at breaktime and hold my hand through the fence. Eventually, the school told her she had to stop this, and I was inconsolable.

My lovely cousin Angela, who was in the big school next door, looked out for me after that. For the first few months of my school days she would give up her playtime and her own friends to stand on the other side of the railings, while I just looked at her with my big pleading eyes, never speaking. Throughout my life she has helped me through my times of loss and pain.

Eventually I adjusted more to school but even then the only place I really wanted to be was at home in the kitchen with Mam or with the rest of my family and friends, running and playing on the lovely green slopes around Rivington.

The top of Hope Street runs straight onto the road that leads up to the beautiful countryside of Rivington and the Pike. As a family we would often walk the country lanes and wander down by the reservoirs where the bluebells grew, visiting the ruined castle that Lord Leverhulme had transported from Liverpool and re-built brick by brick. In those pre-health and safety days, I would think nothing of climbing and running along the top of the battlements and jumping across gaps high above the ground. We had so much fun scrabbling around the ruins and we would then make our way to one of the barns for fizzy pop and toffees. For centuries, on Good Fridays, the mill and factory workers would walk for miles in a spiral round the hill to the top of the Pike, to re-enact the last journey of Jesus Christ. It is a local tradition to this day, and at Easter hundreds of people still walk in procession round the hill.

The countryside around Rivington occupies a very special place in my heart, not only because it is beautiful and connects me to something greater in the way only nature can, but because it holds special memories full of love and laughter. Even as a baby I used to love going out there. I am told that on Sunday mornings, while Mam had a lie-in and then made the Sunday dinner, my dad would push me up Lever Park Avenue to Rivington, with my brother toddling alongside with one hand on the pram. Later, Mam and us kids, and Auntie Alice and her son Howard, would all trail up to Rivi, as we called it, with them chatting all the time, as mams do, and us just running wild for the hell of it. When I got a little older and the mams were working, usually in the mills, long summer days were spent up there in a gang of us kids who would leave home in the morning with our jam butties and return at the end of the day for tea – sunburned, dirty, happy and tired. As the youngest I was probably a bit of a nuisance who tagged along, but my memory is that we roamed happily in feral packs through days that seemed endless and utterly carefree.

My abiding memories of Rivington are of lush green landscapes with bright sun in the warmth of summer, or a blanket of white snow with a bright blue sky overhead in winter. We would be wrapped up warm on those snowy days but would get hotter and hotter as we hurtled down the white slopes on our home-made sledges, making black tracks in the snow. I would go so far as to say that Rivington is not only alive in my mind, but that it is actually a part of me and flows through my blood.

Our house sat on the edge of Horwich, about fifteen minutes' walk from the centre of town. As a young child my favourite place in the town centre was the indoor/outdoor market, the hub of community life every Tuesday and Friday. Me and Mam would walk the length of Hope Street, and at the bottom turn into the lane with a row of shops leading to the centre. On the way we would pass Little Grandma's house on Spring Gardens, and pop our heads round the door to ask if she needed anything. We would then go to the end of Grandma's little row where, on the opposite corner to the haberdasher's was Porky Markland's bacon shop. The shop window had trotters lined up next to a pig's head staring out at us on a plate. The butcher slaughtered his own pigs and two or three of them would regularly be led past Grandma's house, screeching pitifully as they went to meet their fate in the back yard of the shop. Angela remembers going from Grandma's across to Markland's with a jug to be filled with warm milk from freshly milked cows. By the time she got home her mouth would be covered with the telltale signs of cream from the top.

A little further up from the house on the lane was another shop, run by Rosie the grocer. She was loved by all because she gave tick even though more often than not she didn't get it all back. She had the only coffee grinder in town and the delicious smell of coffee beans filled her shop. Tick wasn't available everywhere but there were always the moneylenders who came weekly to collect their high-interest payments. Pawn shops flourished in those days, too, and it is a sign of the times that one has opened up again round here just recently.

When we reached the market, Mam would hold my hand tight in the crowds and I had to be very patient as she stopped to talk to everyone we met on our way. As well as the regular food stalls there were stalls selling shoes and bedding, cards and books. My favourite was the underwear stall where lots of shiny plastic legs in seamed stockings were stuck upside-down with their toes pointing in the air. Alongside there were piles of ladies' knickers, enormous ones that came down to the knees with elastic at the top and bottom. Dad called them passion killers! They also sold liberty bodices, the vest-like garments with buttons that we kids had to wear for about eight months of the year.

On our way home we would stop off at Grandma's again to deliver the shopping, and we would usually stay for a brew. I don't remember being part of their conversations, just sitting beside my mam and feeling close to them both. Grandma would give me a spoonful of malt extract while I was there. Unlike the malt and slippery elm that Mam made me eat 'for my own good', Grandma's spoonful was sweet, gooey and delicious, and I had no trouble getting it down.

Little Grandma lived just off the main shopping lane, in an old blackened, L-shaped, stone house. Two other cottages had been built around this original building, which had stood alone before the coming of the railway works. On one side of Grandma lived a family in a two-up two-down, and on the other side, on the corner of the lane, was the habadashery shop run by two spinster sisters. All three properties shared a back yard in which there were three brick toilets.

Three steep, scrubbed and pumice-stoned steps led straight into Grandma's front room. Your eyes were immediately drawn to the fire on the left. The fireplace was a large black range with a little round hob for the kettle. The fender came out about three feet and on each corner there was a little seat where cousin Angela and my auntie Joan would perch. Facing the open fire was a hard, uncomfortable sofa made of horsehair, and the floor was covered by an old, patterned oilcloth, cracked and faded with use. In front of the fire there was a rag rug made out of old coats by the women in the family. In those days, worn-out coats would be cut into little oblong pieces and put into colour groups. The women would sit at each corner of the rug with a little tool and work their way into the centre, matching the colours and pulling the rag pieces through the hard net backing while they chatted.

Facing the front door on the back wall was an old oak dresser, which was the second item to catch your eye because half of it was missing. The dresser had two drawers, the bottom one used by the cat to sleep in, and at either side of the drawers, where there should have been two doors, there were gaping holes revealing all the jumbled contents normally kept hidden from sight. The doors had provided a few hours' warmth for the home when money was too short to buy coal. On top of the drawers was a fine-looking, polished wood gramophone. It had a handle at the side that would make a whirring sound as you wound it up to speed. You then placed the arm with the needle carefully onto the spinning vinyl record, and songs would come out of the trumpet. This luxury item had been given to Grandma by a doctor for whom she used to clean. When he emigrated to Australia he gave it as a gift because he knew that Grandma's youngest, Joan, loved to sing.

To the left of the oak dresser was the door into the small, cold kitchen and pantry, which overlooked the back yard and lavvies. Here there was a stone flagged floor which Grandma 'red-raddled' to a sheen on her knees. This red cream came in green and blue as well, depending on your preference. In the kitchen were two wooden chairs and a table, and the children would have to eat standing up while the adults sat down. There was a gas ring on a cupboard that hid the gas cylinder. There was no electricity and downstairs was lit by gaslights that were lowered by a chain. A little box with a white mantel would be bought from Buchanan's, the hardware shop, and carried to Grandma's home carefully as it was very fragile. It would be placed in the light fixture and lit with matches, which would make the mantle harden and glow brightly. The light would then be hoisted back up to the wooden-beamed ceiling.

Upstairs there were two very cold bedrooms lit only by candles. In the summer the house kept cool, but in the winter Grandma, Angela and Joan would be forced to sleep together for warmth. Not having damp-proof courses, the stone walls would be running with water and it was so chilly you could see your own breath. A striped, horsehair mattress lay on the bed, on top of which lots of old army coats were heaped. This was the sole bedding. The coats were very heavy yet they were still not enough to keep out the cold.

Making our way home from Grandma's we would have to walk through the busy centre of our bustling village community. Here were the butcher's, the chemist, the Co-op, the second-hand shops, the baker's selling bread and hot pies, and the still-surviving ironmonger's with its distinctive smell, a strange but wonderful combination of paint, compost, adhesives, wood and rubber. These shops nestled between the many pubs, the public hall, the picture house and the doctors' surgeries. At the top of the lane was the railway station, accessing Bolton, Manchester and the local towns. Another cinema was situated at the bottom of the lane. At one point, cinema was such a huge part of local, and indeed national, culture that even a small town like Horwich could support three picture houses: the Palace, the Picture House and Johnny's in the arcade. Alongside the dance halls and church socials, cinema was a great source of entertainment and escapism with its promises of glamour, excitement and romance. The big names in my childhood included Jean Harlow, the platinum blonde bombshell, and the good-looking hero Alan Ladd. These stars and the characters they played could not have been more removed from the tough lives lived by working-class people in an industrial northern town.

I am sure I must have been to the pictures in Horwich more than once but the only occasion I can bring to mind is the time me, my brother and Dad went to the cinema but never got to see the film. Just as the lights were dimming and I stared at the big screen in eager anticipation, Dad suddenly announced, 'Come on, we're going.' Not at all happy with this directive I starting to play up and Dad had to yank me along, saying, 'Shush, shush, get down.' The three of us had to creep up the aisle, bent over double and holding hands, until we were out in the daylight we'd left behind only minutes before. Once outside, Dad looked behind and said 'Run!', so we did. We had no idea why we were running but were absolutely terrified about what might happen if we stopped. We ran till we could run no more. Eventually, panting for breath, we came to a halt at the top of the lane. Dad looked back to see if we were being chased and, much to our relief, we were not. We never did find out why someone was after him but it was an unforgettable outing to the pictures.

Half a mile down from the centre of Horwich, over the bridge towards Bolton, are the loco works and the mills. When I was young nearly everyone in Horwich worked at the mill or the loco works, which made and repaired railway locomotives. In the 1950s there was still a big church-going culture of all denominations and Horwich's many churches were dotted all around the centre of town too. Most have survived, but a few have been converted into restaurants. The Protestant parish church looks down on the village from its position on the top road and affords the best view of Rivington Pike and the moors. Traditionally, this is where the well-off lived in their large houses.

Down past the market is the Catholic Church, with a beautiful statue of Mother Mary in the garden. She looks out straight ahead and there, directly opposite her, is the Spiritualist Church. The doors of each church face each other across the main road, separated by a zebra crossing marked with beacons, which I have always thought highly symbolic. The Catholics were brought up to fear Spirit communication and told never to enter the Spiritualist Church, but nevertheless many have crossed that road and received help and understanding in the Spiritualist Church without feeling their Catholic beliefs were at all compromised. The Spiritualist Church is a place where all are welcome.

Interestingly, I have also felt drawn to the Catholic Church at times, and when visiting Ireland I frequently attend the Catholic services there. I love the mass and the supernatural teachings of miracles, healing and angelic beings in the Catholic religion. I have always thought these two religions are not too dissimilar.

The Spiritualist religion is based on seven principles of universalism. One of the most renowned and respected advocates of the early Modern Spiritualist Movement was Emma Hardinge Britain. She was a powerful medium, who in 1869 channelled the 'Principles of Spiritualism' from Robert Owen, socialist reformer and co-founder of the Cooperative society, who had died ten years earlier. The 'Seven Principles of Spiritualism' were published in 1887, and have endured through to the present day as the foundation stones of Modern Spiritualism. These are:

1. The Fatherhood of God

2. The Brotherhood of Man

3. The Communion of Spirits and the Ministry of Angels

4. The Continuous Existence of the Human Soul

5. Personal Responsibility

6. Compensation and Retribution Hereafter for all the Good or Evil Deeds done on Earth

7. Eternal Progress Open to every Human Soul.

We attended the Spiritualist Church as a family. There were many services including a Divine Service on Sunday evening and Clairvoyance and Healing services throughout the week. As a young child I also went to the Lyceum service – a Sunday school based on what Andrew Jackson Davis, the American pioneer Spiritualist, had seen on his travels to the Spirit world. Inspired by what he saw Spirit children doing, we were taught how to do the calisthenics – what we know these days as aerobics. We did these routines for about thirty minutes with the grown-ups, marching and exercising to music together. It was great fun and created a real sense of well-being. Though it is nothing unusual now, this type of group fitness class was unheard of then. It was especially good to do this with our Mam and Dad and to feel that we were all part of the Church together.

After the calisthenics, us children would separate from the adults and have a service in which we learned about the Spirit world and how our little Spirit guides look after and help us. As I had been brought up with Mam telling us about our Spirit guides, I really felt at home. We were also taught how to behave with love and respect – and how to sew, write poetry, draw, sing and dance. Unlike ordinary school where children were often put down and humiliated, at the Lyceum children were encouraged to think creatively and our ideas were regularly complimented. We were really made to feel as if what we had to say was important, and for those of us who were shy or lacking in confidence this came as a tremendous boost.

Furthermore, we were repeatedly reassured that help was always on hand from our Spirit guides. My mam gave us the names of our little guides; mine was Laura and, later in my teens, a boy called Peter. These were children who had already passed over. Their purpose was to help and support those of us still living on the earth plane. I loved these little friends. An excerpt from the Lyceum's *Pearls of Wisdom* handbook illustrates perfectly the mission of our little Spirit guides:

> *As they are early taught that by helping others — if done unselfishly — they help themselves, they are ever ready to offer the helping hand to those weaker than themselves; this develops the soul and advances them in their spiritual condition toward that higher knowledge to which they ever aspire and strive; in a word, they unfold as a rosebud opens to the sun, or the petals of the lily unclose to the light of day, as they become purer and truer, higher and holier, they assume a form of perfection and beauty.*

In the Spiritualist Church children are named rather than christened and I was officially received into the Church in this way. The Naming Ceremony is delightful and can be done at any age. The minister cradles the baby or stands with the person to be named and says the name that they have 'received' from Spirit. The congregation of family and friends each come to the front and offer a flower to the child, who now has their own Spirit name. Mrs Sherrington, or Aunt Lily as we came to know her, was the minister who named me Joy.

There were several services that we regularly attended at the church. The Divine Service, held on Sundays, was an hour of worship starting with a Prayer to the Divine, said by the medium who was to conduct the service, followed by a hymn and the Lord's Prayer. The medium would impart words of wisdom either inspired by Spirit, or by life experiences that had influenced his or her spiritual path. This is a lovely and inspiring feature of the service and was always my favourite part.

Another hymn would lead into the Clairvoyance Service, in which the medium would bring evidence of the survival of loved ones from the Spirit world. The medium was directed to various people in the congregation and passed on personal messages from discarnate friend and relatives. The service always ended with prayers of healing and gratitude to Spirit, and a final prayer: 'Lord, keep us safe this night, secure from all our fears, may Angels guard us whilst we sleep, till morning Light appears. Amen.'

Like most Spiritualist churches, ours also had evenings of clairvoyance, a Development Service and a Service for Healing.

The evening of clairvoyance was similar to the Divine Service, but with little or no words of philosophy. Prayers were always said, but on these evenings the time was given to evidence of survival after death and the continuation of love and Spirit.

The Development groups trained people in mediumship before they went onto conducting services. This training included gaining knowledge on the principles of Spirit communication and how it works. Stilling the mind of its constant chattering and interference in order to 'receive' purely is probably the hardest thing to do and can take many years before someone is proficient. The developing mediums gave and received from each other and their Church members until they were ready to join an established medium who, with the help of Spirit guides, would become a mentor and invite them to join them in services. We would often see visiting mediums at our church, as they would travel to other places so that they could give evidence to people they didn't know.

Finally, we would often attend the weekly Healing Service. Healing is very much a part of the Spiritualist movement. The service would start with prayers, and people wishing to receive healing would sit before one of the healers. Again there was always a Leader of the Healers who taught and made sure the healers followed guidelines regarding the appropriate methods for hands-on healing. Like trainee mediums, healers called upon Divine Spirit to heal through them, and have to train the mind to be still and a clear and pure channel.

Like all the churches in town, our church would sometimes hold parades. We would be costumed in lovely coloured dresses made by our close family friend Auntie Lily on her Singer treadle sewing machine. The Spiritualist banner with its angel motif would be held proudly aloft as we paraded through the streets. We were never ashamed of our religion; it was a part of who we were.

But life at the church was not all about striving for spiritual perfection. There was a lot of larking about too. There were frequent socials, dances, suppers and shows, and in one of these shows I was to play a fairy. My job was to herald the arrival of the group by saying, 'Here come the fairies!' But I had problems with this and no matter how many times I tried, I kept saying, ''Ere cum fuuries.'

Mrs Sherrington had a friend who taught elocution – so I was promptly bundled off to be taught to 'talk proper'. Unfortunately all that stuck in my mind from the sessions was: 'Daddy's Caar is a Jaguaar and Paar drives raarther faarst. Caarstles, faarms and draaughty baarns, we go chaarging paarst.'

Now my dad only had a push bike! Needless to say I haven't had much call for this through the years (although I did learn that posh people put an 'r' in nearly every word where there aren't any). Unsurprisingly, on the night itself I went on stage and still said, ''Ere cum fuuries.'

Everything I learned at the Spiritualist Church complemented what I had been taught at home. Kindred spirits from the church would come to our home for sittings. There was a solid core of seven regulars at these sittings: Mam, Dad, Little Grandma, Angela, Mam's cousin Edith, her husband John and my cousin Martha. Edith was a handsome, curvy woman with dark features and curly black hair. Glamorous and flamboyant with a powerful voice, she looked to me like a film star and sounded like an angel, singing both on the club circuit and closer to home at local socials. Her husband, Uncle John, was a lovely man with twinkly blue eyes who was always very kind to us children, devising little quizzes and games for us to do.

This core group of seven at the sittings were all related by blood or marriage to Johanna, my great-grandmother who came from Africa. They were a close-knit group, with everyone getting on well together. The sittings were the focal point of their lives.

Originally, Mam had started doing table tapping at Little Grandma's house, with Grandma and Angela joining in. After Mam and Dad got married they started table tapping in our kitchen, with Dad joining them. This silent waiting for the table to move helped Mam to develop into the gifted trance medium that she became. When she went into trance Spirit told Mam to invite our relatives, and they started doing regular sittings in the kitchen, moving into the front room when the circle of seven was well-established. These sittings started in 1947, a year before my birth, and were to continue until we left Hope Street some seven years later.

I started joining in the circles myself from the

age of about six. I used to be fascinated watching my mam go into a trance and seeing how she took on the characteristics and voice of whichever Spirit was trying to get through.

The sittings would start with a prayer and a hymn, usually 'Abide with Me'. Then the circle waited quietly for Mam to still herself sufficiently to create a perfect channel for the Spirits to enter. It never failed to amaze me when it happened, watching, hearing and sensing their personalities work through my mother. At these times she was not my mam, just a pure and clean instrument for Spirits to enter and give their messages fluently. I was in awe of proceedings during my first sittings, but all the other sitters were very relaxed and at ease with the light-hearted atmosphere, which caused the best possible vibration for Spirit to come through.

Strangely, never once in all the years of the sittings were they interrupted by anyone, even by our lovely neighbour Doris who very regularly came to have a natter or to borrow a cup of sugar. It was as if Spirit created the best possible environment for us. The house was a lovely sociable place for the sitters and the Spirit friends to visit.

In the early sittings, there were a lot of physical phenomena connected to Spirit. This was almost certainly because my dad couldn't help asking for proof.

One night a couple of friends of ours joined

Mam, Dad, Angela and Grandma for a sitting. Dad had confided in them about Mam's mediumship and they'd asked to attend. The woman had been a bit nervous, but curiosity got the better of them and along they came. The woman was edgy but managed to settle down, say the welcoming prayer and wait for Mam to go into her trance state. They had been waiting for longer than usual and Mam still hadn't gone through, when out of the silence and darkness a bright silver orb shot across their heads at high speed. The woman leaped up out of her chair screaming and the sitting couldn't go on. The couple never came again so whether Spirit did this to deter them or whether the woman had somehow created the phenomenon herself through her fear and negative energy, I don't know. My dad maintained the Spirit friends were protecting Mam, because if this lady had panicked when she'd been in trance, it could have been dangerous for her.

Dad told me of another physical manifestation that occurred some time later when the sittings were more established. Dad and the women in our family, Mam, Grandma, Edith and Angela, were sitting in silence in the circle when a beautiful white carnation with pink edging slowly lowered from the ceiling. Dad stood up and plucked it from the air to find that it was still covered with dew and had the most exquisite perfume. My Dad pressed it and kept as a keepsake for the dark days ahead.

One day Mam and Dad were in the kitchen and

Dad must have asked for some physical proof yet again, because the tea towel that hung on a hook by the cooker just lifted up and floated for a little bit. Then it slowly dropped to the floor. After that, Dad hung it up and knocked it off no end of times to see if it could happen by accident but there was no way it could have floated like that on its own.

On another occasion my mother was physically protected by Spirit. When I was at school one morning my mother came downstairs to find herself enveloped in a white, smoky substance so thick she couldn't see the walls. She said that she didn't feel at all afraid, just comforted and protected. Eventually, the smoke – what we now know as ectoplasm – evaporated, and things returned to normal.

Later that morning my cousin Angela came flying round in a panic to tell Mam that Grandma wasn't well and that Billy, her youngest son, wasn't doing anything to help. They set off and on the way the mist fell again around Mam's head, though not as thick, and Angela said it remained there all the way. When Mam saw Billy sprawled on the sofa, she gave him a piece of her mind, and told him to get the doctor. Not one for being told what to do, Billy promptly jumped up and punched her hard in the face. Angela witnessed the blow and said that the force should have sent Mam flying to the ground. But although Mam was traumatised and unsteady, and her face was badly marked, the injury was far less than it should have been. There was no doubt that this misty substance had protected her that day.

The doctor was eventually called and Grandma recovered enough to be left with Angela, but what was interesting about that episode was Mam's reaction to Billy. My dad was all for going round there and sorting him out when he got home from work, but Mam wouldn't hear of it. She knew she had been protected by Spirit and this was the only thing that mattered. She didn't want the cycle of violence to continue.

Most of the Spirit friends who came through my mother were people who had died in the previous century and they would tell all about their lives and their passing to Spirit. They spoke of the great joy they had felt at being met by their loved ones, entering into what they sometimes called the Summerland. They told of their many wonderful experiences as they were shown around the Spirit realms.

A common theme that emerged was how much more alive they felt than when they had been on earth. They often said they now felt as if they had been asleep for most of their lives.

Some, who had experienced long illnesses or had a traumatic passing would require a period of healing slumber in the Domes of Light where they were cared for until they would awake, transformed and revitalized. Spirit people were magnetically drawn to a particular realm through the law of attraction. The newly arrived would be drawn to like-minded people who shared their values, aura colour and level of understanding. It seemed to me that it was so much easier to live in the Spirit world than on the earthly plane, but my mother was always at great pains to impress upon me that we create our own environment through our thoughts and attitudes on earth as well as when we pass over.

Many of the Spirits became friends of long-standing. One of the names I remember mentioned regularly around the kitchen table was Miss Johnson. For a while we speculated she was Amy Johnson, the female aviator, but later we learned that she had worked in psychic research before she died. Miss Johnson was a lifelong guide to my mam and would always come first to introduce the Spirit visitors to the circle. She acted as a kind of guardian along with another Spirit we knew as the Cobbler, a gatekeeper to protect Mam from harmful Spirits. Miss Johnson had a beautiful well-modulated voice and sounded like a kindly headmistress.

As for the Cobbler, he never came through the sittings to speak himself. We heard about him only from Mam and the other Spirit friends. His job was to ensure that only those who were of the right vibration were allowed to come through. I have a picture of him in my imagination from my mam's description, in which he is of a slim build and above-average height. I see him in Victorian clothing, a coarse shirt and trousers held together with a leather belt. Mam said he walked with a limp. When I picture him in his last incarnation he is in an old-fashioned workroom sitting behind a shoe anvil, hammering and repairing boots, with a kindly, quiet and diligent air. He himself looks almost in a trance state, lost in his work. Perhaps my image of him in his earthly life prepared him for his work as the gatekeeper to Mam in the Spirit world. Certainly, out of everyone who came through at that time, he had the most important role. Mam had a great affection and respect for him and he was at her side throughout her life.

It is hard to recall all our Spirit visitors because there were so many. The Witchdoctor was fantastic fun and he loved to scare and tease my Dad. When he first came through he would do a dance and chant. He was very agile and moved quickly. I cannot imagine Mam doing that dance of her own volition and even though I was there and saw my mam's body, I was not aware of her at all, just the Witchdoctor dancing.

There was always a lot of banter and laughter between Dad and the Witchdoctor, and they had a great relationship, taking enormous pleasure in each other's company. The Witchdoctor had a stick that he would pretend to poke my dad with while making strange tribal sounds. The energy would be light-hearted but he really did have a powerful presence. On one occasion Dad told me the Witchdoctor was doing his customary poking and teasing routine when Dad jokingly stood up to fight. My mam was not a big woman, but working through her the Witchdoctor lifted Dad up in the air as light as a feather.

Other regular Spirit visitors were Stephen, his sister Betty and their father, whom we called 'the Spirit Doctor'. Stephen and Betty were relaxed and chatty with us but their father was more formal. Stephen was one of my favourites. He was charming and made everyone feel special and interesting even though our lives must have appeared dull to him after his most recent incarnation. He and his sister Betty had been London socialites in the twenties and thirties. Stephen had been a keen mountaineer and was killed this way.

The family were all very well-spoken without any kind of regional accent – what used to be known as a BBC voice – although they each had their unique personalities and diction. Stephen was more laid-back but confident. He was interested in everyone and everyone liked him. He would ask everyone how they were and made everyone present feel valued. He and his sister Betty were very close when they were together on earth and they remained so in the Spirit world. If Betty came through in the circles she followed Stephen's lead. Betty was very friendly and more excitable than

Stephen and they had a sort of sibling banter going on between them. Their father, on the other hand, was very formal in his speech, mannerisms and communication. He had been a highly respected doctor on the earth plane and he came to offer advice and treatment on health concerns.

Grandma loved coming up to the sittings with Angela. They must have been a breath of fresh air and much-needed period of respite in her hard and stressful existence. Throughout her life she loved talking to the Doctor. She didn't have a strong Lancashire accent and her vocabulary was better than the rest of the family's, thanks to the private education that her mother had been able to provide for her. Talking to the Doctor seemed to give her strength and took her back to a time when she would communicate with the really 'well-off' – albeit on the telephone through her job at the Horwich Exchange. She could easily have been accused of having 'airs and graces' but, like her mother before her, she had been educated and had known a very different lifestyle in her younger days. I remember Grandma often saying the word 'fruition', which sounded lovely although I didn't know what it meant.

A visit my Grandma could never stop talking about was the time when Queen Victoria came through. Grandma told me that everyone watched speechlessly as Mam's stature changed before their eyes. She became very upright with a regal bearing and, amazingly, even Victoria's famous bustle physically appeared at Mam's back and her clothes turned black.

It wasn't a long visit. She stopped just long enough to greet the sitters with a brief nod of her head before she was gone. As Grandma described it, my mother's transformation happened gradually until she was standing in front of them looking just like the Queen Victoria she had remembered as a child.

It is known that when Victoria was plunged into grief at the death of her husband, Albert, she took to Spiritualism in an attempt to make contact with him. That may go some way to explaining her appearing to us.

I also remember hearing about the rather touching story about two young German soldiers who had died in the Second World War. Fearful of the response of the sitters, Miss Johnson came through first to ask them not to judge or be angry with the young men. The soldiers, Siegfried and Carl, found it very difficult to talk about the war except to say – in their strong German accents – that they had no choice in doing what they did. My dad and the other sitters treated these two young men with compassion and understanding, and a real and lasting friendship through Spirit was formed. They started coming just before I joined the circles but were still there once I become an established part of the group. I was struck by how different they were. Carl was very gentle and shy while Siegfried was a more confident character altogether.

The vast majority of our visiting Spirits were just ordinary folk in Spirit form. I remember one lady with a very strong Yorkshire accent who had been a weaver in the mill. She was incredibly loud and sounded as though she had no teeth when she spoke, which made us laugh.

But what I remember most vividly from those early days is not one particular Spirit friend or sitting, but the atmosphere of joy and laughter that surrounded them. There was no sense of any malevolent force or of playing with darkness, just a wonderful sensation of light and love. The Spirits impressed upon us that everyone on earth has a guide, or angel if you like, but that some people are so wrapped up in negativity that it is difficult for Spirits to get through. Help will always be there if asked for, however. The moment a request for help is made, the angels are there. Our small group would sit and listen in wonder, amazed at our privilege in having such communication and insight.

The sittings had started in the kitchen but later, when the circle was well-established, they moved into the front room. The front room was used exclusively for the sittings, and by this time the sitters were very relaxed and happy with the visiting Spirit friends. In fact there would be much laughter as they were encouraged by Spirit to sing, do little sketches and be happy. Looking back I have no doubt that all these things were meticulously planned by Spirit in order to create the right atmosphere for what was about to take place.

In 1953, when I was five, Spirit informed Mam to call the sitters to a special circle. Mam was told that there were some very important things to impart concerning the world. The group gathered long after my brother and I had gone to sleep so that they would not be interrupted. They were serious, excited and expectant, but nothing would prepare them for what they were about to hear. They sat in a circle, and as usual they started by singing Dad's favourite hymn, 'Abide with Me'.

By this time Mam's mediumship had developed into a clear and pure channel for Spirit to come through. The sitters had dedicated so many hours to Spirit that it would only take about fifteen minutes for her to enter the deep trance state necessary for the communion to commence. Miss Johnson always came through first to introduce the evening and the visitors who were to come. The Cobbler, Mam's Spirit gatekeeper, would be by her at all times, ensuring her safety.

On this night, Miss Johnson introduced the waiting group to an astounding concept called 'The Work'. The things they were told left this little group of ordinary working-class folk absolutely amazed. In fact it's no exaggeration to say that the things they were about to hear would become the foundation and focal point of their lives from that moment on.

The Work, they were told, involved the reincarnation of souls. This had been going on for several centuries. The sitters, along with many others, had lived many times before and had returned time and time again to the earth plane to bring about The Work.

The Work was nearing its completion and very soon the two worlds would come together in what was described as 'the twinkling of an eye', but only when the time was right. The veils between the worlds would disappear and heaven on earth would be established. When this happened the sitters would 'come into their own' and know what to do without being told. They would also lead others to 'go through' into this new world when the time was right.

They would be at all times guided by Spirit, and throughout their lives they would be led to meet other reincarnated Spirits who were here for The Work also. They would instantly recognise these people through a feeling of extraordinary and powerful love. It was such an ancient bond that the feeling would be unmistakeable.

Running parallel to the final manifestations of The Work would be many natural and man-made disasters. However, the sitters must keep faith in The Work at all times. It was also at this significant sitting that the concept of 'thought is a living thing' was particularly stressed.

We can only imagine what this group of ordinary people felt like after the circle. This was nearly sixty years ago and very few in Britain had heard about reincarnation, let alone a group of working-class folks in Horwich. To be told that they had been born time and time again in order to bring about The Work was incredible. Who can blame them for feeling special and desperate for The Work to start?

I am not sure if it was this sitting when what we came to call the 'The Voice' first came through, but the sitters always thought of The Voice as Jesus. Certainly the group came to understand that Jesus was the head of The Work and of the circle.

The group was told they had to keep The Work secret as it was not for the public domain. If they had said anything anyway they would have been thought mad. We might take reincarnation for granted now or at least have heard about it, and we might now have more understanding about the power of thought. But back then, these things were unheard of.

It was in this way that the concept of The Work entered the consciousness of a very ordinary but dedicated group of seven people. As a young person I had often wondered why our family had been chosen to receive the wonderful experience and knowledge of the Spirit world and of The Work. Our family had made many mistakes and hurt people, just like everyone else. We were just very ordinary poor common people.

Of course I now know that we were no more 'chosen' than the rest of humanity. It was just that my mam and the rest of the sitters had dedicated their lives and energy to Spirit for many years. Thus, they had opened a channel into a frequency that always has and always will exist until the two worlds join and become one. This frequency is constantly present, just waiting for us all to 'tune in' when we choose to do so.

Obviously, at the age of five I did not understand all this – it was only much later that it began to make sense to me. But I was always aware of The Work – there was never a time when I did not know about it. It was part of my being as I grew up.

But life wasn't all about Spiritualism and the miraculous. My Mam made sure we kept our feet on the ground and lived as normal a life as possible. We were fed, sheltered, clothed and loved. When they could afford it, the odd treat was thrown in too. Despite my parents' interest in Spirit, it was in every other respect a very normal childhood.

Although they could be very loving and close, Mam and Dad had their differences, often about money. I saw all the laughter and affection between them but I also heard the rows. Back in the 1950s men ruled the roost when it came to money. They held the purse strings while the women had sole responsibility for the domestic duties at home, looking after the family. Most domestic rows round our way started at teatime on pay day, when the men came home with their pay packets, and our household was no different. Pay days were always tinged with worry and sadness. Dad would come home from the works and reckon up what Mam had spent her housekeeping money on the previous week and what was needed for the next. Of course there was often a big gap because she always overspent. She was frequently extravagant, buying herself and Grandma stockings and make-up from the market, treats for us kids, or something new for the house. Dad was very careful with money and a row would invariably break out. If Angela was around she would whisk me and my brother into the front room and try to distract us by telling stories of fairies and goblins, but it was hard to concentrate and these times could be very upsetting.

I was about six when I realised that all was not well between my parents. I only began to understand the reasons for the break-up and what had happened much later. When I began to research my family history I began to understand, too, not only how deep the fault lines lay, but also, more importantly, how Spirit had been working through our family for many generations, guiding us towards the revelation that was The Work.

But first I needed to understand where Mam's special gift came from. I was aware that Little Grandma had a very unusual background, and that there were several interesting stories surrounding her mother, my great-grandmother. I started to dig deep into my family history to find out more. It seemed I came from a long line of spiritually aware women.

Part Two

The Family Saga

I began to research our family's history when I discovered an old school notebook in which my mother had written an account of her own early life and her gift. It made me curious to know more about where her gift had come from, and in particular more about my great-grandmother, a figure of mythic status in our family. When it came to researching her history, the traces of her life were sparser and harder to piece together – there are very few official mentions of her apart from one in a booklet about the Horwich Telephone Exchange. But gradually, collecting all the anecdotal evidence, I began to build up the story of this remarkable woman.

I have seen very little physical evidence of my great-grandmother except for one photograph brought over several years ago from a relative in Ireland. In the photo a stately, Victorian lady stares out. She has high cheekbones and is strikingly beautiful – and unmistakeably black.

Johanna de Lange was a mixed-race woman from Dutch South Africa, the daughter of a white Dutch settler and a black African woman. She was born into a wealthy South African Boer family and raised by her paternal grandparents. They not only had money invested in the diamond mines but also owned a big stud farm called the Orange Free Stud.

They bred horses and, we believe, ostriches too. It is said that Great-grandmother used to ride a black stallion, and her black nanny, to whom she was very close, used to talk about her riding the 'big black devil'.

Johanna's grandfather was a doctor and it was perhaps because of his encouragement that she trained to become a nurse. There is speculation in the family that her real mother was in fact her nanny, and it seems to be true that Johanna never forgot her and talked about her throughout her life.

There is no way of knowing if Johanna was treated as well as her white cousins by her grand-parents, but at least she was not cast out for the shameful sin of being a 'half-caste' as she almost certainly would have been several decades later in the time of Apartheid. She was raised within the strict teachings of the Dutch Reform Church and knew every word of the Bible, but stories that my grandmother, her daughter, used to tell us – and I will tell you – convince me that she also had Spirit running through her.

In 1876, Johanna married Dirk Van Heeswyk and they had a son, Richard, who was born in 1884. But by 1886 she was on her own again, either through separation or the death of Dirk, and it was then that she met my great-grandfather, Martin Joseph Chaisty.

It has been possible to trace my great-grandfather's

movements with rather more accuracy than Johanna's. His parents, Martin and Catherine Chaisty, left Waterford in Ireland as part of a wide-scale emigration and arrived in England in the late 1850s. They settled in Hulme, Manchester, and it was here in 1863 that their third son, my great-grandfather, Martin Joseph, was born. In the late 1860s, the family moved a few miles down the road to Gorton, also in East Manchester, where records show that Martin Sr worked as a labourer. He may well have moved so that he could get employment at Peacock's Loco Engineering Works. It is equally likely, however, that along with much of the rest of the Irish Catholic community in the area, he would have volunteered to work on the magnificent Gorton Monastery. Work started on the monastery in 1861 and was not completed until 1872. We think it is very likely that Martin Sr would have been involved in helping the friars with the construction, which included hand-making all the bricks on site from clay excavated from the foundations. In the evenings, one of the friars, Brother Patrick Dalton, would visit all the local pubs and social venues in the area, asking for a penny for a brick. In this way he collected a good bit of money towards the building costs.

Consecrated in 1873, Gorton was the largest parish church built in England since the Reformation, a tremendous structure of cathedral-like proportions that was visible from miles around.

Designed by E.W. Pugin, son of the famous Augustus Pugin who designed the Houses of Parliament, Gorton was a magnificent example of high Victorian Gothic architecture and widely regarded as Pugin's finest masterpiece. Later dubbed Manchester's Taj Mahal, the church was created for a band of Franciscan friars from Belgium who had arrived in this unremarkable suburb of East Manchester in 1861 to serve the local Catholic community. Peacock's, the local engineering works, was expanding rapidly in the late nineteenth century, and the influx of Catholic immigrants from Ireland meant that Gorton's congregation grew from three hundred to six thousand within a few short years. The friars built three schools in the grounds of the monastery and had their own band, choir and dramatic society as well as youth clubs and football teams. Martin Junior would almost certainly have received his early education and spiritual instruction from the Brothers.

At the age of sixteen (though we think he lied about his age to get in), Martin enlisted in the Royal Navy, and on 12 December 1879 he became a 'Boy 2nd Class' on board the HMS *Impregnable*, a school ship based in Davenport. Although he was only stationed on board the *Impregnable* for eight days until 20 December, he received a five-pound Christmas payment. On 21 December he was transferred to serve on board the HMS *Implacable*, a battleship of the 'Formidable' class. He served with the *Implacable* for just over eighteen months, when in June 1881 he was moved to the HMS *Lion*. He'd joined the *Implacable* as a 'Seaman 2nd Class', but moving to the *Lion* he was now a 'Boy 1st Class'. On 15 September of that year he was promoted to ordinary seaman. During this time his character and conduct was shown to be 'good' and 'very good'.

The 1881 census has him serving on board the HMS *Royal Adelaide*, stationed in Davenport. This is likely to have been a training vessel, and in January 1882 he was transferred to the HMS *Thalia*. In his late teens he sailed to South Africa. He served on the HMS *Boadicea* and the HMS *Flora* until his discharge on the Cape in April 1883.

We have no clear record of his movements between his discharge and marriage, though there is some suggestion that he worked on the railways. We do know that he became seriously ill in Kimberly on the Cape and was tended back to health by his beautiful, dark-skinned nurse, Johanna De Lange, with whom he promptly fell in love. They were married there in 1886.

Johanna's grandfather disinherited her for reasons that are not entirely clear, though we can fairly safely assume that he disapproved of her union with Martin. But she stuck by her red-haired Irish sea captain and chose love over money. It was a courageous attitude for any woman to take at that time when opportunities to support oneself were so rare, even more so for a woman of mixed race. Nothing daunted, Johanna and Martin quickly went on to have two children. Martin Junior was born in Cape Colony in 1887 and Lawrence was born in Natal Province in 1889. Martin also raised Richard Van Heeswyk, Johanna's son from her first marriage, as his own.

Early in 1891, the family decided to return to England and travelled on board the SS *Drummond Castle*, arriving in Southampton on 21 July 1891. My grandmother told me that when Johanna set sail for England she brought with her lots of ostrich feathers to give away, possibly in a bid for acceptance in a foreign land. My 'Little Grandma' Hettie, Johanna and Martin's daughter (born later in England), said that her brother Lawrence always walked with a swinging gait, because he was just learning to walk when they were on the *Drummond Castle*, which was not very large and pitched and rolled severely in heavy seas. Interestingly, the ship ran onto the rocks in thick fog off the coast of North Wales and sank five years later.

I feel very proud to have had a black great-grandma, a pioneer who set sail over the seas to follow her heart. I was brought up not to be a racist and was fascinated by great-grandma's story, which I had known all my life. But the story did not end with their arrival in England.

After they landed in Southampton, Martin brought the family north to Horwich. It is thought that Martin and Johanna decided to settle in Horwich because Martin had a brother who had moved here and found employment at the locomotive works.

The Horwich that they now called home was undergoing a huge transformation thanks to the Industrial Revolution, which was transforming the North. Fifty years earlier it had been a small crossroads village on the road between Bolton and Chorley. But it had one important asset that set it apart from other such villages: an abundant supply of clean, fresh water from the Pennines. This is an essential ingredient for two of the North-West's traditional industries, cotton milling and bleaching. The bleach works and a couple of mills supported the 3500 or so people who lived in the parish, but by the end of the 1870s these two industries were in decline and the future prospects for Horwich were looking bleak.

In 1884, however, the Lancashire and Yorkshire Railway Company bought a huge plot of land just to the south of the village and started building their locomotive works. In the six years that followed, the population of Horwich snowballed to 12,500. Hundreds of new houses had to be built for the influx of workers now pouring into the village. The old Horwich infrastructure couldn't cope and new shops, banks, bakeries, butchers, pubs, parks and schools opened in the village to serve the swelling population. Extra roads were needed as well as a new sewage treatment plant, and in just over five years Horwich was transformed from a sleepy village into a small industrial town, becoming not only much more prosperous but also developing into a much stronger and more sociable community. The old brickworks, a paper mill, and quarries were re-opened, and Horwich found a new lease of life. A new weaving mill was built and in 1889, almost five years after the construction of the loco works started, and shortly before Martin and Johanna arrived, the first locomotive was delivered.

It was into this newly prosperous Horwich that Martin and Johanna, now calling herself Annie, settled in the autumn of 1891 with their family. They found a home at 102 Lee Lane, renting a two-up, two-down right in the centre of the town. Martin found employment in the loco works and Johanna settled her young family into this traditional working-class community. My grandma Hettie was the first of their children to be born in Horwich in 1893, followed four years later by her sister Ellen. In 1900 the last of their children, Albert, was born.

Johanna was the first woman of colour in this northern town and although this was in the days before racial prejudice took hold, she would have held a certain fascination for the locals. But it wasn't just her skin colour that made her stand out.

Although my great-grandma had been brought

up as a Christian by her Dutch grandparents in the Cape, and later attended the Catholic Church in Horwich, her deeply personal relationship with Christ and the world of the supernatural was distinctly African. Her Spirit had to find its expression. Johanna could quote the Bible almost word for word in her strange accent, but her African blood added an exotic twist to her form of Christianity. With her nursing experience she quickly became the respected local midwife, and Grandma said that she also worked as a healer, further proof that she had Spirit as well as religion. Her faith in God, in Spirit communication and her healing ministrations were the foundation of her life and actions.

My grandmother remembers Johanna as a superstitious woman, shaking salt on the doorstep if they had received a visit from somebody she didn't like. Practices like these may have been one of the reasons why one Sunday her husband Martin marched the entire family out of the local Catholic Church, never to return. Martin was possibly intolerant of the local church's strict teachings because he had been nurtured as a child by the Franciscan brothers who had been compassionate, open and kind.

Communication with the Spirit world was seen as the devil's work by many in the Church and speculation as to the reason for the Chaistys' sudden departure ranges from Johanna's healing practices to the fact that they didn't send their children to Sunday school. Both actions would have been frowned upon by the Church. Either way, my grandma recalled that Martin was a hothead, and moves like this were not out of the ordinary.

In that one decisive gesture my Grandma and her siblings were freed from the control, fear, guilt and dogma of nineteenth-century organised religion. A small branch of the Irish Catholic community in Horwich was effectively released from the Church and given free rein to commune personally with the divine. Future members of the family would now be free to deepen their relationship with Spirit, and continue their search for esoteric knowledge. In this way the stage was set for a remarkable medium, my mam, to enter this free-thinking and spiritual family two generations later. She was to bring with her a profound message of world-changing proportions.

Martin and Johanna had six children in total to raise, plus there was also a boy the same age as Albert called Fred Wate, who was recorded on the 1911 census as adopted and living with them, though we don't know anything else about him. My Grandma Hettie was the middle child. Johanna was a very busy woman, not just bringing up her large family and working as the local midwife, but also running Horwich's new telephone exchange too. Leaving their rented home in 1902, the family moved across the street so that Johanna could take over the running and management of the local 100-line telephone switchboard that had been set up in the front room of 97 Lee Lane. The building is still there, but today it is a florist.

Running the exchange was considered quite a prestigious job. Most women in those days worked in the mill, so the job of telephone operator was a glamorous one, all the more of an achievement for a black immigrant. It was still a relatively new technology in those days: the telephone itself had of course been invented by Alexander Graham Bell in 1876, but it was not until 1879 that the first telephone exchange was opened for the public in the UK in Manchester. Only businesses used the telephones in the early days, and by 1889 Bolton still had only ninety-six subscribers, nearly all of whom were commercial users. The cost would have been prohibitive to most people but slowly this method of communication became more widely available.

Interestingly, A.G. Bell, the inventor of the telephone, was an early Spiritualist. Spiritualism was part of the great movement of the time to integrate science and spirituality, and many leading scientists thought it should be possible to measure spiritual phenomena in the same way scientists were learning to measure the physical world. The nineteenth century saw the beginning of the integration of the intuitive Spirit mind and the material scientific mind, starting the journey from innocence to experience which continues today.

For me, the story of Spiritualism is inextricably entwined with that of my family. Although it is a largely forgotten part of Britain's history these days, the Spiritualist Church has been around for generations, and of course mediumship and Spirit communication is nothing new. The supernatural has pervaded every sacred text and practice of humanity since time began, and continues openly and naturally to this day in those places where it has not been forced to stop by incoming religions.

In eighteenth- and nineteenth-century America and Europe, Christianity remained the dominant religion. But these places were also a melting pot of ideas influenced by Eastern religions, secret doctrine and mysticism, as well as the new science and materialism. William Blake, Emmanuel Swedenborg, Rudolph Steiner, and many other intellectual mystics who have communed with Spirit and angels, led the way for ordinary folks to have a more personal communication with the Spirit world, bypassing the priests and organised religion. Abraham Lincoln and his wife even held séances in the White House.

America, of course, proved to be a natural home for Spiritualism and the movement flourished there in the nineteenth century. Founded on the high ideals of freedom, equality and esoteric doctrine, America also had a shameful past, with its history of slavery and genocide of its indigenous people. These manifestations of the opposite ends of the spectrum of the human condition reflect our innate drive to bring about light and unity into the world while at the same time being equally driven by fear and greed. It was no wonder that so many Americans turned to Spiritualism in an effort to act from the Spirit mind rather than the material mind.

It is also interesting to note that at this time many of the Spirit guides who were teaching through the mediumship of white Christians appeared in the form of recently departed indigenous Americans, in other words they were the souls of Native American victims of genocide. Now freed from the oppression of the physical realm, these ancient ones could come into their own once again in the land of Spirit and, still being close to the earth, could shine their light and knowledge onto their younger brothers and sisters, who were intent on doing away with the old and creating the New World.

Researching this book I discovered an extra-ordinary connection from this time between the Manchester area in which we lived and these Native American Indians who were so important to Spiritualism. In 1887, Black Elk, Medicine Man of the Oglala Lakota (Sioux) tribe, came to England and lived in a tipi on the banks of the River Irwell in Salford for six months, while he was performing in *Buffalo Bill's Wild West* show at the Belle Vue.

I was amazed to read Black Elk's letters home speaking of his time in Manchester. On 15 February 1888, Black Elk wrote:

Now I will tell you about how I am doing the Wild West show. Always in my mind I hold the law and all along I live remembering GOD. But the show runs day and night too, so at two o'clock we quit. BUT all along I live remembering God so He enables me to do it all [. . .]

Here the country is different, the days are all dark. It is always smoky so we never see the sun clearly.

A condition of joining the show had been that all the Native Americans had to have Christian instruction. Most of them were on the run after the Battle of Little Bighorn in 1876, in which General Custer had been killed, so they had gladly signed up, whatever strings might be attached. When the show returned to America many of them would be killed at the terrible massacre of Wounded Knee in 1890 (Black Elk himself was injured during it). Some decided to stay, and made Manchester their home.

Black Elk tells of his first meeting with Queen Victoria when he danced for her at her Golden Jubilee celebrations. He was still only in his early twenties when he was chosen for his good looks and skilled dancing to be one of five to dance at the celebrations while he was in England in 1887. According to his account the Queen made a speech to them, saying that, 'All over the world I have seen all kinds of people . . . but today I have seen the best-looking people.' Black Elk tells us that she shook hands only with the Indians in the show. Later she rode by and everyone bowed to her, but she turned and bowed only to the Indians.

But to go back to Johanna's story, by the turn of the century Johanna was still working at the telephone exchange and life was going well for her. By the standards of the era she was an ambitious and strikingly independent woman who paid for private education for her two daughters, my grandma Hettie and her sister Ellen. This was a very forward-thinking thing to do at the time and virtually unique among the working classes. Clearly Johanna and Martin were unusual and independent-thinking parents. They also paid for piano lessons for their girls, and Grandma – who had learnt the instrument herself as a child – loved to play Chopin whenever she got access to a piano. In fact in later years Grandma used to hold musical evenings on Saturday nights, in which she would play the piano, her young nephew Geoff would be on saxophone and her niece Alwyn Maie would sing jazz tunes.

The children were unusually cultured for their time and class and it seems that Johanna was determined to give them the best of everything.

My grandma's life was so promising and hopeful when she was young, a bitter contrast to the abject poverty in which she would later live.

Information from the census tells us that Martin was living with Johanna in Horwich in 1901, but that by 1911 he had moved to Derby. He and his son Martin Joseph had taken lodgings with a Nellie Johnson and he was working on the railways as an oxy/acetylene welder. We don't know if Great-Grandfather's marriage to Johanna had become strained but it appeared that a deep affection remained between them. On their twenty-fifth wedding anniversary in 1911, Martin sent Johanna a card that said: 'Married 17 January 1886. From husband to wife Annie [they were known as Joe and Annie sometimes]. Twenty-five years have gone, since we united as one, and although we are apart we are still together in heart, as we were when we first made a start. With eternal love from your loving husband, Martin.'

But whatever the reasons for their separation, it was a bald fact that he left my great-grandmother Johanna back in Horwich to raise their family of six children alone.

Still, Johanna made the best of the situation, looking after her children and carrying on with her telephone work. When they got a little older, Grandma Hettie and her sister Ellen often helped their mother at the exchange and I remember that my grandma would become quite animated when she reminisced about those days. She said she loved the job of telephonist, talking to the well-to-do around Horwich and Rivington, and having these important people calling on the telephone in the house. The switchboard itself was actually in the front room.

In fact, Johanna's telephone exchange was to play a part in the story of one very prominent local resident, William Hesketh Lever, who was to become one of the great northern nonconformist heroes of the era. Born in Bolton in 1851, William had worked for his father's small grocery business as a boy, cycling to nearby towns and selling soap from his bike. It was probably on one of these trips that he fell in love with Rivington. With his astute business mind he went on to establish an industry manufacturing soap, which later became Unilever, one of the most successful businesses in the United Kingdom. In 1911 he was made a Baronet, taking the name Lord Leverhulme. He was a businessman, a Liberal and a philanthropist who pioneered improving conditions for the working classes before the Great War.

In 1900 William Lever bought the Rivington Hall estate and Noon Hill on the moor behind Rivington Pike. In early 1901, he set about building an enormous bungalow on the side of the moor just below the Pike. Prefabricated out of timber in Bolton, the bungalow was built in a matter of months and in November of that year he announced that

Roynton Cottage, with its newly installed telephone, was to be his summer home.

It should have been a peaceful family haven for the great man, but it was not to be. Just twelve years later, on 7 July 1913, my great-grandmother Johanna was roused at about half past one in the morning to take urgent telephone calls to summon the fire brigade. Royton Cottage was burning fiercely. Calls were put through to both the Horwich and Chorley fire stations, but neither brigade turned out as Rivington was not in their area. By the time help arrived, the cottage was beyond saving, and by morning it was a smouldering ruin. All that remained were the chimney stacks, some blackened beams, the brick dovecote and entrance porch. Fortunately, Lord and Lady Leverhulme had not been at home that night. They were attending a reception for King George V and Queen Mary at Knowsley Hall, the home of the Earl and Countess of Derby, and had left the cottage earlier that day. They did not hear about the fire until later the following afternoon.

It was quite clear from the evidence that the fire had been started in several places simultaneously, and that this was no accident but a deliberate act of arson. In fact it turned out that the fire had been started by someone in the suffragette movement. A small dispatch case was found near the ruins containing a typewritten message that read: 'Lancashire's message to the King from the women:

Votes for women due. Message to the King, Liverpool: Wake up the Government. First give us a reason to be loyal, and then try us.' The case also contained a pair of ladies' gloves, one of them blood-stained.

The search for the culprit ended on 10 July when Edith Rigby, the forty-year-old wife and daughter of two prominent Preston doctors, presented herself at a Liverpool police station admitting not only to the arson attack, but also to an earlier bomb explosion at the Liverpool Cotton Exchange. In her statement she said that she had instructed her chauffeur to drive herself and a male sympathiser over to Rivington and, making sure no one was there, they doused Lord Leverhulme's cottage with paraffin and set fire to it.

When the women's suffrage movement was at its height, Lancashire women were the most radical of all. Emmeline Pankhurst, her two daughters, Sylvia and Christabel, and the former mill girl, Annie Kenny, ran the new radicalised 'Deeds Not Words' campaign for women's suffrage from Emmeline's house in Chorlton on Medlock, Manchester. Clearly Edith Rigby, a previously respectable woman willing to discuss and demonstrate peacefully, was a convert to this new campaign.

Mrs Rigby was sentenced to nine months' imprisonment on 30 July, and promptly went on hunger strike. She was released a week later to recover her health, then re-arrested. This cycle of imprisonment, hunger strike, release and re-arrest became known as 'Cat and Mouse' and was shamefully adopted by the establishment to avoid creating martyrs of the suffragettes. But it inflamed an already volatile situation and radicalised previously peaceful supporters of the women's movement. Between July and October Edith Rigby was released and re-arrested three times.

The irony of this story is that Lord and Lady Leverhulme were staunch Liberals and ardent supporters of the right of women to have the vote. They worked tirelessly to improve conditions for their employees, with their most famous achievement being the creation of Port Sunlight, a model village of eight hundred individually designed homes, built between 1899 and 1914 on the Wirral to house workers from Lord Levenhulme's nearby soap factory. An unprecedented architectural and social achievement for its time, its properties were then, and are still now, highly desirable. Lady Leverhulme was responsible for the creation of lavishly landscaped gardens in accordance with the values of a garden suburb, influenced by the ideas of William Morris and the Arts and Crafts Movement. She saw to it that Port Sunlight had its own schools, churches, art gallery, open-air swimming pool and even a cottage hospital. Lady Leverhulme also encouraged recreation along the lines of literature, art, music and science, and claimed that her husband's aim in creating Port Sunlight was 'to socialise and Christianise business relations and get back to that close-knit family brotherhood that existed in the good old days of hard labour'. The workers at Port Sunlight were educated, looked-after and paid well, as long as they conformed to Lord and Lady Leverhulme's paternalistic guidance, worked hard – and didn't drink! There was a temperance bar on site to further this aim.

Most workers complied willingly, persuaded by the good wages and unparalleled working conditions. On the workers' children's birthdays, Lady Leverhulme would travel in her horse-drawn buggy to deliver a classic children's book as a gift. Not surprisingly they were enormously loved and respected by their workers. Leverhulme later became a Liberal MP and championed the National Old Age Pension, a provision he had already made for his own workers.

Three weeks after the fire that destroyed their home in Rivington, Leverhulme's beloved wife of forty years died of pneumonia while he was away on business. Childhood sweethearts, Elizabeth and William had even attended the same school in Wood Street, Bolton together. Leverhulme poured all his grief into getting their home rebuilt, but this time from more durable brick and stone. He promised that his house, which he would open to the public, would 'rise as a phoenix from the ashes'.

He improved the already landscaped grounds with a lovely terraced Japanese garden, waterfalls and pagodas. He had a gymnasium installed and even a mechanical horse, which after his bath would provide exercise and shake him dry at the same time! In 1920, when Leverhulme was about seventy, he built a famous ballroom in an effort to recapture his youthful love of dancing and perhaps to provide himself with female company. He grieved for Lady L, and sorely missed the love of his life, but still craved the companionship of women, asking his son if it would be inappropriate to have friends and dance again. Having gained his son's approval, he set to and built this opulent glass-domed ballroom with beautiful furnishings and a sprung dance floor which, when not in use, was covered in an enormous Persian carpet.

Around this time, while Lord Leverhulme was attempting to recapture his youth, my own great-grandfather was undertaking an adventure of his own. It was then that Martin travelled to Canada, visiting his son Martin Jr and daughter-in-law Lillian. We do not know exactly when they emigrated to Canada, but when Martin visited them they were living on Victoria Island, British Columbia. We have a photograph of a smiling Martin halfway up a mountain.

There is a story in the family that Johanna planned to visit him and had booked a passage on the *Titanic*. The tale goes that she received a premonition of the disaster, and refused to board the ship when it sailed, but her luggage was already on board and sank with the liner. On trying to check this story, it appears that there were thousands of people who claim to have booked to sail on the *Titanic*, but changed their minds at the last minute! So it seems this story may well have grown in the telling into an accepted piece of family folklore. Who knows the truth of it?

What we do know is that when Martin returned to England, his daughter-in-law Lillian and her two children, Ellen and Norman, came back with him for a holiday to visit the family in Horwich. Lillian must have been heavily pregnant at the time, because when she returned to Canada eight months later, she travelled with three children. Baby Lillian was then six months old.

In 1913 Johanna and Martin's daughter Hettie, my grandma, married William Smart. She was twenty-one and he was twenty-three. The union was a happy one and they were in deeply in love. However, they were destined to face many hardships together.

The Great War broke out within a year of their marriage and we know that Granddad joined up because we have photos of him in uniform. We also know from his sister Polly's daughter, Auntie Alice, that when he came home from the army he was never really well. Hettie and William had seven children, three of whom died. Their first baby,

Oliver, died in infancy. Their daughter Dolly was killed by a horse and cart aged eight, and Eva died of diphtheria at the age of four.

Martin's daughter-in-law Lillian was in Horwich at the time Eva died, having arrived for another visit with the family. She had six children by this time: Ellen, Norman, Lillian, Richard, Martin and Winifred. Incredibly, Norman, Richard and Martin all died at Fall Birch Hospital on the same day, 1 May 1920, from the diphtheria outbreak that had just killed Eva. They are all buried together at the parish church. Although death from diphtheria was not uncommon at the time, to lose three sons on the same day seems unbearably cruel.

When Lillian set sail to return to Canada she travelled with only three of her children.

But life continues, despite the tragedies, and on 28 November 1922, Grandma Hettie gave birth to my mother, Evelyn. Born into a free-spirited family, Evelyn was listened to when, as a young child, she started to 'see' and communicate with Spirit children. She was not made to fear and close her mind to these beautiful visions and communions with the Spirit friends that would walk with her throughout her life. She was brought up free from dogma and religious conformity and her gift was encouraged to flower.

However, there was much hardship to be borne within the family as Evelyn grew up. After demob her dad, William, was employed at the bleach works until he became suddenly ill with acute stomach pains in 1926. He died soon after in hospital of a burst duodenal ulcer. So at the age of thirty-four Grandma had lost her husband and three of her children. At the time of William's death she was in hospital herself with pancreatitis and couldn't even attend the funeral.

It was left to their eldest daughter Annie, then nearly nine, to attend the funeral on behalf of her mother and help look after the little ones: one-year-old Billy, four-year-old Evelyn, and Leonard who was seven. Annie had been promised a bike for Christmas from her dad but she never did get one and that was an abiding memory for her. She had been so excited, looking forward to Christmas.

My mam's last lovely memory of her dad was of being carried by him through the Japanese Gardens on one of Lord Leverhulme's open days to the public. Even though she was very young when he died, my mam really loved her dad and he often came for her during sittings to take her on travels into the Spirit world.

Grandma still had a little bit of money after her husband's death. We don't know if it was a life insurance settlement or some kind of payment from the bleach works, but either way it soon went, and they were plunged into terrible poverty. Life was very hard and Grandma, who no longer had an income, had to rely on charity. On one occasion a charity representative in a suit called to search the cupboards and, finding a tin of peaches, stopped the money from his church on the grounds of my grandmother's extravagance. In fact, the family suffered frequent hunger throughout my mother's childhood. They would hide behind the couch when the rent man came, fearful that they would be thrown out for not being able to pay. There was not, as there is now, the safety net of the welfare state to keep you fed, housed and warm.

Grandma's own mother, Johanna, was now in her sixties and living with her son Lawrence in Bolton. She died three years after her son-in-law in 1929 at the age of sixty-eight.

Meanwhile, life continued to be hard for Grandma. She was regularly forced to move her children from place to place due to debts and her inability to pay the rent. Arriving home from school on one occasion, my mother and her brothers and sister discovered they had been thrown out of their lodgings. They had to trail around the streets of Horwich to find their mother, who was frantically looking for a new place to live.

Schooling could be a brutal experience for poor children too. Often hungry, my mam could not concentrate at school and the teachers often treated poor, fatherless children with disdain. Consequently, Mam grew up innately clever but uneducated. Such things would perhaps not be allowed to occur today but not so long ago it was all very different. My Auntie Alice remembers going to see my grandma and her family when she was little. She said they were so poor she was given a cup of tea in a jam jar.

Despite living in desperate poverty, Grandma still found time to nurture her faith in Spirit by attending meetings at 'The Rooms', as she insisted on calling them, with Auntie Polly, her late husband William's sister. These meetings were held in an upstairs room above a hall in Horwich that was the forerunner of the Spiritualist Church I attended as a child. I remember Grandma saying that there was an afternoon service and a lot of mothers would go when the men were working and the children in school. Visiting mediums would come and give messages from the departed. She said the locals used to call these meetings 'the Spooks'.

It is no surprise that Auntie Polly would attend with my mam as there were Spiritualist links on my grandad William's side of the family too. Polly and William had another brother called Ben who was a medium and was known for 'walking' with tables as they started to move with the force of Spirit.

In fact there were many pioneer Spiritualist mediums around at this time who would have paved the way for people like Ben and my mother to follow. Maurice Barbanell was probably the most famous British trance medium and one who has left a huge legacy. Maurice was born in 1881 to Jewish parents – a devout mother and atheist father

– in the grinding poverty of London's East End. As a young man Maurice was agnostic but attended a séance out of curiosity. Bored by the goings-on he fell asleep, but was surprised to learn that rather than falling asleep he had actually drifted into a trance state and was 'channelling' Spirit. This was the beginning of a sixty-year relationship and a lifelong dedication to Spiritualism. Maurice Barbanell was championed by Sir Arthur Conan Doyle and eventually joined the home circle of Hannan Swaffer, a Fleet Street journalist, socialist and all-round colourful character hailed as 'the greatest personality that had walked down Fleet Street in our time'. Maurice channelled his guide, Silver Birch, who gave Spiritual philosophy and teachings on the world of Spirit and the relationship with us on the earth plane. There are many books on the teachings of Silver Birch and they are an inspiring read. Perhaps Maurice's most significant achievement was founding and editing the *Psychic News*, a newspaper still in existence today.

Whether the gifts of mediumship are inherited or not, it seems significant that my mother had not just a mother and grandmother but also an uncle with a special relationship with Spirit. Grandma was raised in the supernatural world of her African mother and the Celtic mysticism of her father (who had so memorably rejected the Catholic Church), so she would encourage all her children to go to church – any church – on a Sunday afternoon. My mother's brothers and sisters favoured the Salvation Army, but although she attended a few times, Mam never quite felt at home there. She tried a few other churches but never felt welcome. Eventually she walked through the door of the recently built Horwich Spiritualist Church. There she was greeted like a homecoming queen. They fed her, they showed real interest in what she had to say and taught her practical skills. More importantly they sparked her spiritual curiosity.

Mam felt totally accepted and so began a life-long devotion to Spiritualism. Many years later, in the 1980s, my mother would become the President of the Horwich Spiritualist Church, and would likewise lovingly welcome people into the Church with open arms. But it was the warm reception in those first tentative weeks as a poor uneducated child that were to prove the definitive turning point in my mother's life. Sunday afternoons became the bright spot in what was an otherwise gruelling existence.

In the early twentieth century, Spiritualism had spread throughout Britain and Europe, pervading every class and culture. Great scientific and literary men such as Oliver Lodge, Sir Arthur Conan Doyle and the French pedagogue Allan Kardec, were just three of many eminent minds who were convinced of the truth that lies behind life after death, Spirit communication and the evolution of Spirit.

I have always found it interesting that my mother,

without doubt the most spiritual and gifted of all our family, should have been born not just at a time when Spiritualism was blossoming worldwide, but in the same week that a pioneering minister, Reverend George Vale Owen, was reluctantly leaving his ministry in the north of England to tour America, speaking on Christianity and its obvious foundations in the psychic phenomenon of Spiritualism. He was going at the behest of his great friend and champion of Spiritualism, the author Sir Arthur Conan Doyle. Doyle had been able to contact a son he had lost during the Great War and was a convinced Spiritualist because of it. Interestingly, he lived in Crowborough in Sussex, later twinned with Horwich.

Born in the Ladywood suburb of Birmingham in 1869, George Vale Owen was a remarkable man for his time, a gifted writer and poet who published his first book, *Leaves from the Mental Tree*, at the age of twenty. While researching the history of Spiritualism recently for this book I was privileged to meet David Owen, the grandson of George Vale Owen, at his home with its beautiful view of the Rivington Beacon. Every day he is reminded of the life of his grandfather who was a beacon of hope to so many. David and I spent a lovely morning talking about George and his work to unite the two worlds. We both felt his presence and we know he continues to share his message still. David has written a wonderful biography of his grandfather's life called *When the Angels Say, Write.*

George Vale Owen's call to the ministry was irresistible and in 1890 he gave up a well-paid job in order to study Theology at Queen's College, Birmingham. After completing his finals he married his wife Rose and wrote to the Bishop of Liverpool requesting a job. He was made an assistant curate in West Derby, from where he wrote many articles for the press, pointing out the terrible working and housing conditions his parishioners had to endure. After several more moves and the sadness of losing two babies, George, his wife and their three surviving children were moved to Orford, Warrington.

For over twenty years Owen worked tirelessly to serve his flock. When he first arrived in Orford, services had to be held in the schoolhouse on a Sunday and he would have to put all the furniture back in time for lessons on Monday. After many years of campaigning he gradually raised enough money to build a church of his own. A deeply compassionate and modest man, he was loved by his flock and went beyond the call of duty to serve them, ministering to the many sick in the days before medicine and healthcare became widely available. During the First World War, when the men of the parish failed to return from the battle-fields, he was always on hand to comfort the bereaved. Although he had doggedly maintained throughout his career that his first duty was to the Holy Spirit and God and not the Church, nothing in Owen's career indicated the turning his life would take. A diffident man, he did not go looking for sensationalism and notoriety and was as surprised as anybody when, after the Great War, he began having psychic experiences. He received messages from his mother in the Spirit world who told him of the schools for Spirit children and the beauty of the realms.

Mostly these psychic phenomena took the form of automatic writing, when Spirit would channel the words through him. To begin with his handwriting was shaky and hesitant and the messages often tricky to decipher, but as it continued to come day after day, Owen became fluent and prolific. It just poured out of him. Mostly it was accounts of life after death and philosophical teachings. Lord Northcliffe published these words in his newspaper, *The Weekly Despatch*, in 1920, creating enormous public interest.

Unsurprisingly, Owen was forced out of the ministry by an already furious bishop who considered Owen's work heretical. But by then he had a huge following, and although he was a reticent man by nature, Conan Doyle persuaded him to go on the lecture circuit to spread the message in 1922. Owen's definitive work was the five-volume *Beyond the Veil*. For years he wrote and reflected on the messages he received and on the intervention by

Spirit in his life and ministry. He prayed and studied the Bible and eventually concluded that everything in the New Testament – the miracles, the teaching and healings of Jesus – were in harmony with the teachings and phenomenon underlying Spiritualism. He wrote, 'To me the Christianity of the New Testament and Spiritualism are synonymous . . . Christianity is historically the outcome of certain events which happened two thousand years ago. The principal of these events are psychic phenomena.' Finally, after twenty-five years of communicating with Spirit he told a friend, 'I have been down into the valley of decisions and wrestled it all out . . . I have given myself at last, wholly, to the great cause and any personal feelings count no more at all with me.'

The spiritual baton was passed on to the next generation when Owen's son, the Rev G. E. Owen arrived at the Vicarage here in Rivington in August 1939 with his four children, taking up the post of Anglican minister at the parish church. During his tenure he held a séance where both his father and Lord Leverhulme were present in spirit, as well as the bishop who had forced his father out of the Church, admitting that he had been wrong.

Owen's work set the tone of the age into which my mother was born and it was a very fertile ground for my Mam's deliverance as a medium. Certainly she grew up in an environment that was very supportive of her gift.

Mam talked to me about the early days of Grandma's table tapping at home, which she participated in when she was old enough. She said they would all sit around the table and place both hands lightly on its surface. If there were enough people, hands were spread so that little fingers came into contact with the next person. A prayer would be said or a hymn would be sung and then they would sit in silence and patiently wait. It could take anything from five minutes to a whole hour before their patience was rewarded with the familiar tingling – an electricity, excitement in the air or presence that made itself felt.

When the sensation of Spirit had become unmistakable the leader would ask, 'Is anybody there?' The response would come in several forms: sometimes the table would rise gently on one side then fall, or a knocking on the table would be heard. The sitters, keen to encourage the Spirits, would begin talking to them and the energy would build. Then the table would really start to lift off and drop quickly with force, causing hands to fall off, as if the table were dancing. Sometimes they would walk with it as it moved.

This wasn't Mam's first encounter with Spirit by any means. She had had wonderful experiences with spirit children when she was a young girl, living in a house just a few doors from where the Telephone Exchange had been. Many years later she wrote about her spiritual experience for the

Lyceum and copied the article into an exercise book.

The day I discovered this book in a box of my mam's papers we had put in a drawer, was the day I realised I had to write up the story of the generations of gifted women in my family. This led me to understand how Spirit had been working through our family all this time, and that it was my job to bring this message out into the open.

I had always been aware that my mother was not like other mams – that she was gifted and special – and I had often wondered how it all started out. We take our parents for granted while they are alive but when they are gone we realise there is so much we don't know about them. I am so grateful therefore that a few years before she died my mother wrote the following:

I have hurt many people in my life but I have been hurt also.

I am telling you this to let you see that I am no different to anyone else. I certainly wasn't chosen because I was a goody-goody.

Well, my story starts way back when I was ten years of age. There were six of us, counting my mother who was a widow. My father had left this life early at the age of thirty-six. I was just four years old so I hadn't a great recollection of him.

I was a lively child, not very scholarly, perhaps the reason for this being that instead of listening to what was being said by the teacher, I was worrying how my mother was going to pay the rent. We had very little money but an abundance of love.

I liked my own company a lot, somehow I never felt lonely.

Now I have to explain the layout of our house. At the back of our house we had a large yard. There were a few out-houses scattered around but attached to the side of the kitchen was a big building where I would go into and just mess around on my own. Now, we called this building the cellar and I will explain why.

As you opened the door you walked into a big stone-walled room with flag floors. Thinking about it now it must have been very creepy. My sister and brother would not go into it but I was pleased about that.

Anyway, as you walked into this room at the side of the door, there were about a dozen stone steps leading down into a cellar underneath. I only went down there once – curiosity I suppose, but I didn't like it. There were about six ovens set into a wall – you see, in the 1800s it was a bakery. The smell was terribly damp and it was very cold so I never went there again. But the room above was my haven. I have to tell you this dear reader to give you a picture of what happened.

I must have been going in my room for about a week when it happened. About thirty children, *boys and girls, suddenly appeared, some my age, some younger – happy, laughing, singing and playing games. We would never touch each other. I realise now that I had strayed into their world but at the time it was just something very normal to me and was my secret. I never told my mother or any of the family.*

Well, this went on for about ten months. The funny thing is that we would be together for about half an hour, they would leave and I would go into the house and not think about them until we met again.

Then one day something else happened. We were all playing and laughing when over the top of the noise came the most beautiful singing voice I have ever heard. Suddenly the children disappeared and I was stood alone at the very edge of the stone steps.

The voice was coming from below. Then, floating up the steps, not walking, came the most beautiful lady I have ever seen. Her hair was jet black and long and she had a long white dress on. As she floated nearer to me the dress was billowing out around her.

She was singing a lullaby and there was nothing frightening about her. All I can say is that I was seeing my guardian angel. I ran out of the door and into my mother's arms in the kitchen. To cut a long story short, my mother made me tell her everything but forbade me from ever going into the cellar again.

My mother was a very gifted person and she knew there must have been a reason for the angel's appearance, so she made enquiries as to who had lived there before us. Lo and behold, a young married couple had lived there with a young baby. The young wife, after giving birth, had fallen down the stairs and died. So this was the warning my angel was bringing, because of the stone steps I was stood so close to.

My mother always insisted that Sunday afternoon should be kept for God, so we had to go to a church. Well, my sister and brothers went to the Salvation Army. I tried it a few times with a few of my friends but somehow it wasn't for me. Then I went to the parish church but when you wore clogs and a coat that didn't fit you, this is the time you realise there are two classes. So you learn from a very early age. I did anyway.

Then one Sunday my feet took me to the Spiritualist Church where I was welcomed as if I was royalty and I have been a Spiritualist ever since.

They taught me to read and write, to knit and sew. Alas there are only five us remaining at the church from those happy days.

We have an angel banner over the rostrum and as a child I would gape at this banner and lots of faces would appear on it as they do to this day.

Now I will tell you of my experiences. You will

*have heard of astral travelling, well my first was
many years ago. You remember I told you my
father had gone to Spirit when I was five years
old. The first time I remember travelling was a
feeling of weightlessness and sitting on a train. It
was warm, but there was a gentle breeze.*

*You could put your hand out and touch Love,
it was as if it was solid.*

*You remember I told you my father had gone
to Spirit when I was four years old. Well, I had
this wonderful man sitting at the side of me and
I knew he was my father. We were chatting away
as if we had never been parted. I remember how
proud I was. I had a lovely big picture hat on
my head and a very willowy dress on. Anyway
I was aware that I was in Spirit, but – 'Trains?'
I asked. He explained it was the only way I could
accept my journey, as on this sphere we could
create anything we wished. Since then I have
been with guides but it has been on learning
journeys.*

*The first thing I remember telling my Spirit
guides, was how silly I felt when we moved. I kind
of bounced like a balloon while he and all the
people around me were walking. He laughed at
me and said, 'You must remember, you are only
visiting and have not gone through the veil that
you call death. You can see everyone but they
cannot see you.' He said that they are the same
when they come down to us and they find it diffi-*

cult to stay firm. I then remembered my angel as a child and how she appeared to be floating.

On one of my travels I was taken to a Spirit hospital. I have never known such peace. I saw some buildings and all around there was the greenest grass you have ever seen. People were sat on benches embracing each other. I was told that these people had just left the hospital and their loved ones had come for them. Everywhere I looked, flowers of every hue were spread out like carpets.

In the hospitals there was such peace, not like our wards with their noise, hustle and bustle. Here there was lovely music playing very softly. We went to the laying hospital for shocked Spirits – for example, victims of heart attacks or accidents that had taken them unexpectedly.

The doctors are not in white but are dressed in a special colour according to their progression. Again, flowers are everywhere. There were lovely Spirit men and women sitting by these beds waiting for these passed ones to come round. They came to very gradually, wondering where they were, but they were not afraid as this place was so full of love. Who could be frightened?

This is where the doctors came into their own. He or she would explain to the person via thought transference how they had crossed the river. There must have been a lot more passed between them but I never saw anyone panic or show distress. When they are ready, someone they love is called in to them and a substance comes all around them and you can't see them. This seemed to give them privacy.

Now, more about the flowers. The guide said they were everlasting and that they were the seeds of babies that had miscarried and hadn't breathed on earth. Their substance was too delicate to grow up as Spirit beings so they are everlasting flowers giving off spirituality. They can be taken to your Spirit homes.

I asked why I could see so many lovely Spirits through my mediumship and yet I could feel my family but not see them. My guide told me that they were still working with thought force, and it isn't any easier for them to come than it is for us to visit them. 'Thought is a living language,' he told me, and we should practise it here.

I asked about suicide because someone very dear to me had taken their own life. I was told that they pass over as if they are merely going to sleep, but that when they awaken they would still have to work through their same problem thoughts in the Spirit world.

There are people who cannot accept their passing. These earthbound Spirits link with others of the same mind and they form communities just as we do on earth, but their realm is grey and they are going nowhere. This is where the rescue workers come in. This work is apparently very specialised and takes a lot of power.

They work in groups that are of the same aura colour and they are full of compassion and free from fear. They see love whilst receiving fear and hatred from those in the dark. They move around in groups, never alone, and it takes much training before anyone is allowed to go into the dark spheres. My guide didn't tell me more, although I know there was a lot more to it. I shall have to be patient and wait till I pass over to know more.

I asked about God and was told, 'Use your own thoughts on this one and always have faith in yourself, because this God you ask about is inside you as it is inside everyone in the universe. Live by God's standards, giving love to the lonely, strength to the weak.'

Remember to look within yourselves for the Truth. I have put to paper some of my truths but you, dear reader, must develop your own gifts. Please do: it is possible with faith in yourself and faith in God.

Evelyn.

As far as I know, my mam left school when she was fourteen. Like the majority of young girls with such a limited education, she started work in a local mill. Although the work was hard, dusty and hot, there was a wonderful sense of camaraderie among all the girls that worked there, and she made some good friends.

Her cousin Alice was also working in the mill

then. She and my mam had been to school together and they had always been very close friends. They would often go out shopping, walking up to Rivington, or just parading up and down the lane. She remembers one occasion being chased out of the Arcade and through Horwich by an irate shopkeeper, who caught them peering through his window when he was entertaining a young woman in the back of the shop.

Mam's older sister Annie had married and moved to Blackpool with her husband and their child, Angela, and my mam went to live with them for some time. While she was there she managed to get a job cleaning at the Luis Tussaud Waxworks on the Prom. She started very early in the morning, feeling rather terrified dusting in the Chamber of Horrors all alone, but she loved dusting the Royals and the famous stars such as Douglas Fairbanks, Bing Crosby and Bette Davis. In fact, she was cleaning there one day when in through the doors came some young men from Horwich. For whatever reason – perhaps she felt ashamed of her job – she didn't want to speak to or be recognised by the boys. Thinking quickly, she sat down amongst the waxworks and froze, not moving a muscle, staring straight ahead and not breathing until they had passed. They must have wondered why a cleaner with a duster should have been immortalised in wax!

When she returned from Blackpool my mam went back to live with Grandma, and she quickly found a job back in the mill with her cousin Alice, as a ring spinner. She had not been back at home very long before her sister Annie and her daughter Angela decided to move back to Horwich from Blackpool. With them arrived a male friend requesting lodgings. He was a drinker and aggressive and Mam didn't like him one bit.

This was too much for Mam, who went to live with her cousin Alice. It was a happy time. My mam always said that Alice's family were rich compared to hers, because they had a dad. While she was with Alice she got a job at the loco works. Alice remembers being envious of my mam working there, because it was better paid than the mill. Alice's dad had told her that she was not allowed to go and work there because there were too many young men about.

Mam must have worked at the loco works for a year or two, but found that the atmosphere was not the same as working in the mill. She missed the great friendship, loyalty and laughter she had enjoyed there, so she left and went back to working at the mill alongside Alice again.

My mam was still very close to her mother, and would see her most days. But after a brief spell back at home, she moved again and went to live with Auntie Esther. Esther was not a real Auntie, but a wonderful old Spiritualist she had become very close to at the church. Esther had become my mam's guardian and mentor.

Working at the mill together, Mam and Alice continued to be very good friends, spending their days planning their evenings and days off. They would remain close their whole lives, and when they had both married, Mam and Dad, Alice and her husband Howard would often go out together as a foursome, as it was called in those days, to the pictures or the dances at the De Havilland Aircraft works club, where both Howard and my dad worked then.

However, back in the cold, damp house in Spring Gardens, life continued to be hard for my Grandma. It must have been a tough, lonely business on her own with four children, no husband and no money. There was little in the way of pleasure in my grandmother's life and few of the little comforts that we all take for granted today. Small wonder therefore that eventually she sought comfort in the arms of a man, even if he was married. She became pregnant in 1934, in her early forties, and did her best to disguise it by wearing tight corsets. Nobody knew that she was pregnant, no mean feat considering how closely people lived those days.

When the baby, a girl named Joan, was born, she had deformed legs. Joan spent the first four years of her life in hospital having her legs straightened. She finally came home to live with Grandma in 1939. A story of some kind had to be made up to explain Joan's sudden appearance and to combat the atmosphere of moral judgement of the time, though I am not sure who was told what and when. Certainly the official line was that Joan had rickets.

Nevertheless, Joan's appearance caused a scandal that Grandma never quite got over. There is a family story that Grandma's young nephew and niece by marriage, Geoff and Alwyn Maie, were banned by their mother to attend her musical evenings after Joan was born. But they loved their Auntie Hettie so much that they sneaked there every Saturday nonetheless.

Although times were hard, there was no shortage of love at home, and Hettie kept her children together through thick and thin when it might have been easier to give them up. Everyone who remembered my grandma spoke of her love for her children. But conditions were difficult and, as she grew up, Joan became a strong-minded girl, and there were frequent clashes between her and Grandma's youngest son, Billy.

Billy was a handful for Grandma throughout his life. He had a vile temper, which grew worse with age, and by the time he reached his teens Grandma had become worn out and frightened of him. She loved her son so much but he was impossible for her to discipline. He was inordinately fond of a drink, which only made matters worse, and she didn't have the strength to stand up to him and protect her daughters.

There was a ten-year break from Billy's tyranny when he joined the navy and was then called up to do his National Service, joining the Lancashire Fusiliers in 1947. While he was away there was a wonderful peaceful atmosphere in the house and everybody breathed a sigh of relief. Between tours of duty, he would come back to Grandma's for some leave, which always ended with a squad of soldiers turning up at the house to fetch him back.

Grandma moved from the damp house on Spring Gardens in the centre of Horwich to a two-up two-down over the bridge near the loco works. It was a terraced house, built back-to-back with other terraces behind – one of many built for the influx of workers in the 1880s. It was dry and warm and easy to keep clean and she and the girls were happier than they had ever been. Grandma's daughter Annie had left by this time, but Angela remained along with Joan. So Grandma now had some money coming in from the two girls, who were both working at the mill, and there was enough left for them to keep up with the fashions and to go dancing – their favourite pastime as it was for most young people then.

But it was to be a short-lived respite. Billy returned home on leave on one occasion bringing with him his girlfriend, Queenie, in tow. Queenie was a large, buxom woman with peroxide hair. Billy insisted she should sleep with him in the front bedroom, forcing Grandma to share the back and smallest bedroom with Joan and my cousin Angela. Fearful of her son's erratic temperament, Grandma failed to stand up for her girls yet again and gave in to Billy's unreasonable demands. For Joan, the change was to prove tragic. Within a year she would be dead.

Joan had always had a turbulent relationship with Billy. They were constantly at loggerheads and rowed frequently. This last selfish demand was the final straw. She moved out to live with a relative but, alone and desperately in need of security, love and a place to call her own, she quickly fell in love with local boy, a miner called John. Within a short time she became pregnant. The lovers kept it a fiercely guarded secret, too afraid of the conse-quences if anybody found out. They wanted to marry but John was younger than Joan and they didn't think they would be allowed. Not wishing to be parted, the couple ran away together. No one knew where they had gone and the parents on either side were not able to help them.

The pair rented a flat five miles away in Bolton. I recall as a young child going off in search of them with Grandma, getting off the bus and walking the long St George's Road for hours hoping to spot them. They had been missing for about three months by this time and still nobody knew their precise whereabouts. We returned home defeated and empty-handed.

Several weeks later the police arrived at our house. Joan and her lad had committed suicide together in their flat by gassing themselves. It was such a waste. A local newspaper account of the incident states that two different notes were found at the scene but we don't know what became of them or what they said. Born into shame and secrecy, Joan died that way too.

Whether Joan's suicide was to prove one tragedy too many for Grandma I don't know, but she came to live with us in Bolton when she was sixty-four years old, completely worn out by life. With age, Grandma had become a little disturbed and suspicious of people. She didn't venture out much and turned into something of a recluse. She had a fur coat that she loved to wear in the house. Her hair had once been her crowning glory but it had become very thin in old age and now she wore a brown wig. No matter how poor you were, appearance was important and you made the best of what little you had.

Grandma never really recovered from the multiple humiliations and hardships of her life. Going to collect her pension in the 1960s, she would put flour or calamine lotion all over her face to make herself look ill. She was concerned that if she looked healthy they would stop her money, and however many times my mam assured her the pension was her right, she didn't believe it. Grandma's African heritage had never bothered her when growing up, but with age she became concerned about racism and would avoid the sun. When she died in her eighties, she had seen more than her fair share of hardships and cruelties. Hers was a life of promise unfulfilled, joy not experienced. She had only briefly known happiness in her early life and career, in her first year of marriage before the war and in her relationships with her children, and especially with her granddaughter Angela. She would light up when she reminisced about her private education, her happy times working on the munitions during the war, the early sittings and the wonderful proof they had, and the people who came through. She loved the Spirit friend we knew as the Spirit Doctor especially, and she would re-live the same stories, such as the one about Queen Victoria, over and over again. But brief moments of happinesses always seemed to be snatched away by the next calamity. Losing four children and a husband is not something that can ever really be recovered from but my mother would later go on to feel the Spirit of her two sisters, Eva and Dolly, very strongly in her work as a medium. It must have been a consolation of sorts to my grandma, to know that her children were still around her, albeit in Spirit form.

I don't know how long Queenie stayed with Billy after all the upset but after a while the couple found themselves a house on an estate not far from Hope Street and went to live there. Billy transformed the house from its traditional three-up, two-down layout into something that was almost unheard of then – a spacious open-plan home. He turned out to be a very skilled craftsman. Whether or not these latent skills were recognised and developed in the army, we don't know, but he was able to make almost anything with some simple tools. He knocked through walls, opened up doors, exposed the stairs, enlarged windows, re-plastered and then redecorated the walls with hand-painted murals in the lounge.

Billy and Auntie Alice's husband, Howard, were quite good friends, and Alice recalls one occasion when Howard told her about meeting Billy in the lane. Billy was all cocky and full of himself, declaring to Howard that he was 'now in the big time'. What deal he was supposed to have struck we never did find out. Angela also remembers evenings together when Billy and his brother Leonard used to put on small shows and sketches for them. The format was always the same: Billy was the swaggering Staff Sergeant, and Leonard the poor browbeaten squaddie doing the square bashing and cleaning all the boots. She remembers them as being very funny.

After not hearing from Billy for years, he suddenly reappeared without warning on Mam's doorstep in the 1980s, by which time they were all in their sixties. Billy was homeless and begging for help. Mam immediately took him in, but he was paranoid and had to be sectioned. It subsequently emerged that the poor man was schizophrenic, finally making sense of his extreme behaviour all those years ago. In those early days we'd just thought he was a bit of a bugger who couldn't hold his drink. It wasn't until he was put on medication that he found the peace of mind that had eluded him all his life. When I saw him again it was strange to see how shrunken and pathetic he had become, given how gigantic and terrifying he had once seemed. He spent the last seven years of his life living quietly in a flat in Horwich looked after by my mam, who had a great capacity for forgiveness.

Mam had never lost touch with Spirit through all the family troubles and living with her Spiritualist guardian Auntie Esther must have been a great comfort for her. Certainly her spiritual gifts were to prove a huge magnet to a young man named Arthur Heath, who she met and fell in love with in 1937. My dad knew nothing of my mum's gifts when he first met her – he just saw a lovely-looking girl that he fancied. But he was to be fascinated by her communion with Spirit throughout their marriage. Dad had also attended the Spiritualist Church as a youngster, but their paths hadn't crossed.

Dad liked to reminisce about their first meeting, laughing and shaking his head at his gall. Mum was fifteen at the time and he was seventeen when he saw her walking down the lane. Cheekily, he began singing the hit of the time, 'Too Marvellous for Words.' Years later he still wondered why she had ever given him the time of day.

Dad's father, Arthur Senior, was an engineer at the railway works and a hugely respected trade unionist. He was also a convinced Spiritualist, having had an experience that had left him in no doubt of the power of Spirit. Table-tapping was still popular during the thirties and forties, and during one sitting the news came through that his sister, then living in Bolton, had died suddenly and prematurely. In those days before most homes had telephones, people could only be contacted at work or by telegram. Two days later, Arthur Senior arrived at work to find a letter informing him of her sudden death. Having had such a direct experience with Spirit, Arthur Senior needed no persuading about his son's new girlfriend's burgeoning gifts and he developed a soft spot for this young mill worker.

There is a story that perfectly illustrates Arthur Senior's great generosity of spirit. Upon the death of his stepmother, he inherited some money which, naturally enough, his wife wanted to use to buy furniture. She had only managed to get a dining table and sideboard before the generous and impulsive Arthur Senior had other ideas and started buying drinks and giving the money away to people he thought were his friends. But as soon as the money ran out, the friends drifted away and Arthur

Senior, recognising his foolishness, vowed never to touch another drop of alcohol. From that day until his last he never did.

Unfortunately, his wife, Mary, was somewhat frosty and considered my mother not quite good enough for her son. Arthur had a good job as an engineer like Arthur Senior before him, whilst Mam came from a poor and troubled background. Mam was living with Auntie Esther in a terraced house with gaslight, outside toilet and a tin bath in front of the fire, while Arthur and his family lived in the comparative luxury of a brand new semi-detached council house with bathroom, electricity and a large garden in a secure, stable family unit. This was the house on Hope Street, later to become my home. Mary would have considered herself upper working class while Mam was definitely lower working class.

In the 1940s and 1950s 'class' was of course clearly defined into the categories of working, middle and upper, but there was a very powerful and defining class system within the working classes too, divided according to the type of work the families were engaged in and the level of education, church and social activity. In small towns like ours, everybody knew your business and it was hard to escape bigotry. If someone in your family had broken the rules, everybody in it was labeled – and my mam, with her mother's late, fatherless pregnancy, was no exception.

Nevertheless, Evelyn and Arthur's seven-year courtship was a happy one. They were a very sociable couple, forever going dancing, singing and enjoying time out with their friends. When asked to recall what they remember about Mam and Dad in the early days, surviving friends and relatives mention the laughter that surrounded them wherever they went. They were regulars at the Saturday night socials at the Spiritualist Church where there would be dancing and spot prizes followed by a meat and potato pie supper. At other times they would ramble across Rivington Pike for hours, enjoying the nature and seclusion.

Arthur Senior died early from cancer just before Mam and Dad's marriage in 1944. In those final weeks in hospital before his death, Arthur Senior sometimes saw other patients' beds surrounded by Spirits who had come for them. He would tell his son that they were on their way out and, true enough, within hours they would die.

Arthur Senior's funeral was an astonishing tribute to this highly regarded man and was attended by trade unionists and management alike, who mourned the loss of such a good and generous soul.

My mother, too, felt the blow of his departure. She had lost her champion within Arthur's family and, after their wedding, she and Arthur went to live with his newly widowed mother on Hope Street. There, Grandma Mary made their early married life a misery. There is no doubt that it must have been awful for Mary to lose a beloved husband and then have a daughter-in-law immediately move into her home. But Grandma Mary would insist on instructing her son how a husband should treat a wife, especially one of a lower class, and it didn't exactly endear her to my mam.

Mam was left in no doubt where she stood in the pecking order – and not only in the immediate family. Although some of Arthur's other relatives welcomed her, she was excluded from many family occasions. Arthur, caught between the opposing needs of his bereaved mother and new bride, didn't stand up for his wife as much as he perhaps should have done. Of course that is how my mam told it, but there are two sides to every story. I met Grandma Mary many years later when I was an adult, and I liked her. I see now Mary was simply upholding the values of her generation at a time of huge social change. She was very kind to us and sent my brother and I a five shilling postal order every birthday.

A year after my parents married, Mary met and married a widower, handing the tenancy of the house on Hope Street over to Arthur and Evelyn. For my mother this was to mark the beginning of a much more peaceful phase in married life. This is not to say that Mary didn't still consider Hope Street her home. On occasions she would swoop in unannounced and lay down the law at will. One

Sunday she arrived to find Dad cleaning out the ashes in the grate and hit the roof because that was Mam's job. To top it all, Mam was still in bed, having a lie-in!

From the very start, Dad had always been fascinated by my mam's gift of clairvoyance. The manner in which his father had been told about his sister's death and also having seen the Spirits around the hospital beds before he died had intrigued him. There was an incident one night in the early days of their marriage when Dad, typically, had been hounding the Spirit friends for proof when he was at the Church one evening. During the service he popped through to the back where the loo was, just across the corridor from the kitchen. There was a full moon, and knowing the layout of the church, he had no need to turn on the light. As he walked through the committee room into the kitchen, the moonlight was shining through the window, creating an eerie glow. Suddenly standing before him was his own father, as plain as day. He froze on the spot, his heart pounding in his chest. Tentatively, he took a cautious step forward, then another. As they grew closer, my dad, in a cold sweat and scared to death, said in a very shaky voice, 'Come on, Dad, I'm alright.' Just when he thought they were going to touch my dad bumped into the mirror! On returning back to the service, Mam looked at his ashen face and said, 'You look like you've seen a ghost.'

Certainly, my parents' early marriage was filled with much laughter, and as a child I adored them both. My dad was a loving, protective man with a big heart that he wore on his sleeve. A great lover of life, he had a huge amount of time for people and saw the beauty in everyone. Women particularly responded to him because they could tell that he was genuinely interested in them. This intense curiosity extended to the world at large and he was also a great observer of life. He had a particular interest in politics and trade unionism and like my mother was a passionate socialist. But despite these deeply held convictions he was a light-hearted man and could usually be found telling a funny story or laughing at himself. As a parent, he was all a child could hope for – fun to be with and always there with outstretched arms when we needed comfort. I cannot recall a single instance of him taking his frustrations out on us.

Like Dad, Mam loved to laugh and have fun. She was loving, strong and courageous. She wasn't as sentimental as my dad but she was very insightful and resourceful and would move mountains to help people. She was never afraid to stand up for her beliefs and would always speak her mind. She had suffered a lot as a child and this had made her greatly empathetic to the plight of the underdog. She didn't judge people by their mistakes but rather by the Spirit she saw in everyone. People were drawn to her openness and strength, and in every photo she has her arms around us all. She had grown up facing injustice and poverty and had to fight for everything in her life except for the one thing that really mattered – her innate and life-long faith in God and Spirit. Mam gave us backbone and encouraged us to look beyond the everyday obstacles of negative personalities and petty hurts that can dominate our thinking, and to find the Spirit within us all. Her capacity to love, her knowledge of the Spirit world and her faith were her greatest gifts to her children and everyone she met.

They were exceptional parents and I am truly grateful for their guidance. They taught us to love with all our hearts and to give generously of ourselves. These two extraordinary individuals loved, laughed and lived to the full, experiencing the agonies and ecstasies of this life in the material realm, including falling in love and the eventual breakdown of their marriage.

For sadly, their marriage, forged in love and laughter, was not to survive.

Part Three

Pamela's Journey

I am glad I have reached my sixties and have some perspective before writing about this difficult time in our lives. I am now long since past any need to blame one parent over the other or apportion responsibility for the break-up of their marriage. When we are young, it is easy to point the finger at our parents for everything that goes wrong in our lives, but as adults we all learn how hard life and relationships can be. We can either choose to let the hurt colour our lives and darken our future, or we can learn to forgive and live in love again. And making the mistakes I did in my adult life has given me the empathy and understanding to accept the things my parents did that caused us such pain and loss.

As I have mentioned, there were frequent rows about money, with my father accusing my mother of being a spendthrift. There was also another major row – which seems quite funny now but was anything but at the time – which was caused when the political world intruded on the personal.

My father, like his father, was a trade unionist full of conviction, and I remember well the debates between him and Mam in our house. The 1950s were a heady period for working-class people with a political bent. Even though there was still hardship and rationing after the war, there was an optimism amongst the people. Britain had a Labour government under Clement Atlee that had given birth to the National Health Service, transforming the lives of the working classes who had previously not been able to afford healthcare. Fuelled by the strong political feeling of the times, Dad was committed to making sure that he and his fellow workers were treated fairly by the management at the loco works. Disputes were not an uncommon feature of his working life, but most of them were handled by negotiation and settled without too much disruption.

However, on one occasion when the dispute over pay and conditions dragged on, with neither side being willing to back down, the workers voted to come out on strike. They knew that if they went on strike, they would not be paid, but they went ahead anyway. The company were determined not to give in to the workers' demands and advertised in the local press and on posters for non-union labour to break the strike.

Mam's socialism was sorely tested by this. She was broke as usual, and the promise of good pay and a roll of material for those willing to cross the picket line was too tempting. She was torn between showing solidarity with her husband, and the need to feed her young family. Eventually, disguising herself with a headscarf, she left us with Auntie Lily for the day and, boarding the special bus laid on by the company, went through the barricade where my dad was picketing. Unfortunately he recognised her as the bus slowed down to go through.

That night there was a huge row in the kitchen. My dad was furious that she had been willing to break the strike. But my mam stood her ground, arguing that her need to feed the family came first. For all her strike breaking, Mam was as committed to Socialism as my dad, and, despite the row, in later years they would look back on the incident and have a good laugh about it.

Their faith in Spirit was a huge bond that never faded, but their personal relationship was becoming increasingly difficult to sustain. After seven years of courtship and ten years of marriage, Mam and Dad decided to separate for good, and we had to leave our lovely family home. Mam had become the talk of Hope Street and, unable to live with the constant scrutiny and attention, my mam arranged a council house exchange with a family in Montserrat, Bolton. Although we only moved about five miles, in those days, without a car, it was like living on another planet.

I have often thought about the overwhelmingly sad time when everything in our lives changed. Perhaps it couldn't go on? Were the sitters becoming more involved in the spirit world and forming closer relations with the spirit friends than with their earthly ones? For years they had been prepared in the sittings so they would be ready to receive the higher inspiration, then within a few months of hearing about The Work everything ended abruptly. Perhaps this ensured the purity of the message for the future?

Mam, Dad, my brother and I moved to Bolton just before Christmas, 1954, and ten days later, on 30 December, Dad was gone. They had obviously arranged it that way, and after our last Christmas together as a family, my brother and I were told the news the night before Dad left.

It was devastating.

I can still recall the emotional pain in my chest when my parents broke up, like I had a big hole in my heart. Dad continued to be a loving father from a distance, and every Saturday morning without fail a registered envelope would arrive on the mat. Never once in all our childhoods did Dad forget to send our maintenance.

My brother managed to sustain his bond with Dad and they had regular contact, remaining very close throughout their lives, which was a great comfort to them both.

As for me, Dad used to come up from Luton and visit us about three times a year, but I found these visits fantastically difficult. I would be anxious before he came, knowing that I had to let him go again, and when he did go back it was a huge loss all over again. I would feel heartbroken and would cry myself to sleep every night for a couple of weeks after he left. I had always felt very protective of my dad and I wanted to look after him, even as a very young child. I felt more like his mother than his daughter when we parted and I couldn't bear it when we had to say goodbye.

Eventually I decided to stop seeing him altogether and it was many years later, when I was in my thirties, before we resumed a permanent relationship. If there are any parents out there whose children have chosen not to see them, don't think it is because they don't love you. It really isn't. Keep them in your heart like my dad did, and keep faith that you shall come together again one day.

Several years down the line, Dad remarried and went on to have three more children. He and his wife also became foster parents and they looked after many children, for both long-term and for short-term stays in emergencies. When Dad and I were reunited many years later, I met and came to love my grown-up half-brothers and sisters, as well as some of the foster children.

I am very grateful to have had my dad, albeit briefly. He gave us so much in our few years together, but I understand now that his love and care was needed elsewhere. He had so many loving and fatherly qualities to give, so to be Dad to just two children was not meant to be. His great gift was to share his light and love with as many children in need of it as possible. He did this admirably and I am so proud to be one of those fortunate ones. I believe that no matter how many mistakes and hurts we create in searching for love outside ourselves, it is through that very need and capacity that we eventually find it within ourselves.

But at the time, the move to Bolton was devastating. Not only did we lose our full-time Dad, we lost our friends, our community, our Church and the sittings with our wonderful Spirit friends all in one fell swoop. Stanley, my stepdad-to-be, came to live with us within months of the move and I didn't like him one little bit. As far as I was concerned I already had a dad and I felt jealous of Stanley because he took a lot of my mam's time and attention away from me. My resentment toward him was such that the day they went to get married at the registry office I didn't even get up to see them off.

The summer after their wedding we took a holiday flat in Blackpool. There my mam became ill. To keep us occupied, our new stepdad took us out to play crazy golf. He called me 'Chick' and held my hand and I started to like him. Though my new dad was reserved and not a big talker, he looked after us, and I can never remember him having to shout or show any anger. He had a natural authority to which we instinctively responded – one word from him and we behaved. Over time we became very close and I grew to love him dearly.

During the agonising times after my father's departure I was given a gift from Spirit to help me with my loss. I was alone in our garden when, among all the weeds, I spotted a tiny purple flower. I bent down to look and suddenly everything else disappeared in my consciousness apart from the extraordinary beauty of this tiny flower. My focus became so intense that it filled my whole world. The only way I can describe it is to say that I felt totally at one with the flower; I really 'felt' its beauty intensely and played with it happily as I would another child. It was as natural as that, and I don't know how it started or how long it lasted but it was the most exquisite sensation. I can still feel the beauty and the love when I think about it today. As with all altered states I have experienced, this one felt more 'real' than everyday material reality. These vibrant memories have absolute clarity in my mind and can be called upon and re-experienced at any given time, as if they come from a place that is still living within me.

Because of the move my brother and I had to start at a new school just at the bottom of our road. I cannot remember who took us to school each day. Perhaps we went on our own? But I know that Mam now had to go to work full-time in the cotton mill. She would leave early, around seven in the morning, to catch the bus, and not return until about six o'clock in the evening. I remember coming down the stairs in the mornings when it was so cold I could see my breath. Mam would dress and feed me before rushing off to work. My brother and I were what were commonly referred to as 'latchkey kids' at this time, having to fend for ourselves and do a few jobs around the house after school. One of us would wash up whilst the other did the clearing away of the old ashes, ready for Mam to light a fire when she got in. Afterwards, I used to meet Mam off the bus at teatime, and this was the highlight of my day.

Perhaps I had got used to school by this time, because I don't remember crying the way I used to when I first had to go. Every Monday morning a male teacher would have all the little girls standing on the desks and he would walk around and look us up and down and choose the best-dressed. I didn't like it. His gaze made me feel uncomfortable, and what's more I never won.

Despite my best efforts at school, I never seemed to do well. My brother, on the other hand, sailed through his eleven plus. He was a natural. But I was never jealous of him. He was too lovable for that and I felt happy for his success. I vividly recall Mam writing some numbers on a white hanky and me sneaking it out during a test, pretending to blow my nose and having a crafty look. It didn't help! I still failed my eleven plus. Mam said it didn't matter for a girl as I would soon be married. It sounds awful now but everybody thought that way fifty years ago.

But I do recall loving that final year at primary school. When it rained and I was chosen to go down and help with the little ones during playtime, I would feel very responsible and mature. I would pretend to be a teacher and I think that this was the beginning of my love of working with children, especially those with special needs.

I liked the teacher in that final year class and thought her very nice. But she had an unfortunate habit of picking on a boy called John. She was forever tormenting the poor child, and one day he was made to stand up so she could give him a proper dressing-down in front of all the other children. He turned bright red with humiliation. To this day the one thing I cannot stand is children being humiliated by adults. It saddens me.

In the years that followed, I was often late for senior school and ended up in detention frequently. It was only about half an hour's walk to school or we could easily get the bus, but more often than not I walked to save the fare so I could spend it on toffees or, a few years later, one woodbine and a strip of matches from the corner shop. I still am always last minute no matter how hard I try not to be.

Some Sundays, Thomas and I used to take the bus back to Horwich to see our friends. We loved Auntie Lily, the minister from the Spiritualist Church, and missed our Horwich pals. We would play up Rivi (Rivington Pike) in the morning and then Auntie Lily would take us all to the Lyceum at the Spiritualist Church in the afternoon. Another abiding memory of these times was sledging down the snow-covered hills in the bright sunshine, terrified and laughing, arriving back wet through and getting into real trouble because we were late for Church.

We missed Horwich a lot but we made new friends in Bolton. We played out all the time with the kids in our street and had a lot of fun. Hardly anyone had cars then and we used to play a game called dodgems on our bikes. It was very skilful and you had to stand up, balancing on your pedals and, moving very slowly, try to make the other riders fall over whilst keeping yourself up. The last one standing was the winner. All the kids loved my brother Thomas. He had our dad's gift for entertaining children and would devise the best games. He once started a club and taught us all kinds of interesting things, but I got fed up with always having to make the jam butties. When he started to charge me threepence I promptly un-joined myself from his club.

There are a few teachers that stood out because they *liked* teaching us, and these were the ones I did the best work for. I was especially fond of our English teacher. However, if you misbehaved, all the teachers were very strict. In those days the boys would get the cane on their backside and the girls got it on their hand. It really hurt and was always done by men. In primary school we got the slipper and in secondary school I got the cane a couple of times when detention didn't correct me for being late. I remember standing in the office, holding my hand out, and noticing the teacher's eyes on my chest when the force of the cane made me jump.

I hated it when after exams the results were read out for everyone to hear. I was usually near to the bottom and was always disappointed even though I hadn't really applied myself and shouldn't have been surprised by the results.

I remember the fun we had going to the forests to get dead branches, tying them up with rope to pull them back to the street where we would build our bonfire for the fifth of November. We would make a Guy Fawkes and stand outside shops and pubs, asking for a penny for the guy. On bonfire nights the dads would light the bonfire and the mams would make black peas, tata ash and parkin. We always had treacle toffee and the lads would chuck bangers at the girls.

We didn't have a telly when we first moved to Bolton so it was a real treat to go to my friend's house up the road to watch *Popeye the Sailor Man* after school. Televisions were black and white and quite small compared to today, the screen no wider than about fourteen inches. I remember great excitement when Bolton Wanderers played in the Cup Final and a few of us squeezed into my friend's front room and saw them playing, but we were thrown out for making a noise.

Mam brought my Grandma and Angela to live with us in 1956, when Grandma was sixty-four and completely worn out by life. Our family were under the spotlight again in Horwich because of Joan's suicide.

Because Mam was now having to work full-time at the mill to make ends meet, it was helpful to have Grandma around to look after us during the holidays. I don't know what my stepdad, Stanley, thought of the arrangement. He accepted without complaint, even though he and Grandma evidently didn't care much for each others' company. Perhaps he found her full of airs and graces. But it was nice for us that Grandma was always there when we came in from school. She was on hand to help my mum with the washing and preparing the food, even if she wasn't the greatest cook. She occasionally used to make a cake that sank in the middle and was wet. Grandma called these cakes 'sad', but my brother always scoffed them to please her.

Grandma and Mam used to talk a lot in the evenings and this was the first time that I got to hear anything about Grandma's family history and her early life. I wish now I had paid more attention, because it is a fascinating story and one that has made me very proud of my ancestors.

Mam's circles had stopped for a while after we'd relocated to Bolton, but they restarted in my early teens. I think we only had one every year from when I was nine till I was thirteen, at which point they started up again more regularly. Most of the original sitters had moved away or passed on. So

Great Granddad Martin Chaisty, in his sailors uniform, around 1883, just before he met and married Joahnnna Aledia DeLange in South Africa.

Great Grandmother Johanna Aledia Delange, a woman of mixed race with black African and white Dutch parents. This photograph was taken after she moved to Horwich.

Martin Chaisty Junior. He is the eldest son of Martin Chaisty and Joanna DeLange and he was born in South Africa in 1887. This photograph was taken in British Columbia, Canada where he and his family had emigrated. Soon after, three of his children died of diphtheria on the same day in 1920 in Horwich, while they were on holiday.

This is a 100 line telephone exchange switchboard, identical to the one that was installed in Horwich and operated by Johanna and Hettie in the front room of their home on Lee Lane.

My Grandma and Granddad, Hettie and William (right), on their wedding day in 1913 with my Granddad's sister Polly and her husband.

My Granddad William Smart holding baby Eva during the First World War. She died of diphtheria in 1920 in the same outbreak that claimed the lives of her Canadian cousins.

Winter Hey Lane as it looked in the early years of the Twentieth Century.
The road leading off to the left is Spring Gardens, where Grandma
Hettie lived. This is the house I remember visiting as a child.

Samuel J. Rose's pork butchery shop on Lee Lane, Horwich.

Winter Street party, 1935, to celebrate King George V's Silver Jubilee.

The 'Horwich Spiritualist Church and Lyceum Walk' leaving the church in 1960.

The Guardian Angel banner still hangs in the Church in Horwich. The portraits are of the two pioneers of the Lyceum movement: the American, Andrew Jackson Davis on the left, and his British counterpart, Alfred Kitson, on the right.

The interior of Horwich Spiritualist Church as it is today.

My mother and father,
Evelyn and Arthur, on
their wedding day in 1944.

Rivington Pike casts her protective aura over Hope Street and Horwich.

My mam and dad
dancing in the late 1940s.

Me on a donkey
aged about five.

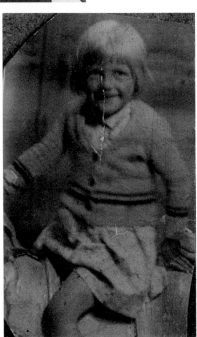

now Mam, Grandma, Uncle John (Mam's cousin Edith's husband), my cousin Martha, my stepdad and I formed the mainstay of the new group. My cousin Angela couldn't come very often as she had young children by then, but I would go and tell her about it the day after. When she did come, it meant there were seven of us again. The evenings were as awe-inspiring as ever.

My brother Thomas, although he had always felt very much a part of the circle, began to drift away from the sittings around the ages of sixteen or seventeen, as the usual teenage preoccupations took hold. By this stage he always had his mates coming round (which was great because I fancied a couple of them!).

The sittings in Bolton were held in our three-bedroomed council house. It was more modern than the one in Horwich. There was a kitchen but it didn't have any atmosphere like our old one, so we never sat in there. Our front room was one big room with a separate dining area, so this is where the sittings were held.

Despite the new surroundings, all the regular Spirits made an appearance – Miss Johnson, Stephen and the Spirit Doctor frequently came through. The Cobbler was always at Mam's side as usual but he never spoke himself. One time my granddad came through, which was very emotional for Grandma. Sadly I don't now recall exactly what was said, but I can remember there were lots of tears.

There were a few very special occasions when the sittings took on a more intense vibration and we would pray and spend time sitting in silence, waiting for 'The Voice' to come through. The entity we referred to as The Voice was highly evolved. He didn't come through like other spirits. My Mam would have to go into a deeper trance than usual and it was at these times that I found watching her most compelling. The group would sit in a circle full of anticipation awaiting the wonderful feeling of love, spirituality and inspiration we knew would follow.

The Voice would always be preceded by what we called the Philosopher Spirits, who would talk of the wonderful changes to come. Although way beyond our understanding in terms of intelligence and spirituality, we were never made to feel unworthy by these highly evolved Spirits. On the contrary, they were loving and full of gratitude for the time we dedicated to them. They made us feel special and said we would be amazed if we realised all we had already achieved. We were told that there would be many natural and man-made disasters, and much turmoil and war in the world, but that running parallel to this would be great and wonderful spiritual changes.

When at last The Voice came through we would be too in awe to speak. Mam's tone would become loud, slow, deep and imposing, but the message would be so full of love, gratitude and compassion that we felt as if we were in an altered state of being ourselves. The atmosphere was profound and we would all feel sacred and beloved, far too in awe to ask questions as we might in an ordinary sitting.

The Voice was very important to our circle. To us he seemed like the word of heaven appearing on earth, but we could never discern any affiliation to organised religion in terms of what he or the Philosophers said. They had progressed far beyond our earthly notions, and were not exclusive to Christianity.

I didn't consider it unusual at the time that a teenage girl should be party to these extraordinary experiences and live such an ordinary life the rest of the time. Occasionally I would find myself wondering if my friends' families had sittings, but for the most part it was just how we lived. I think in all I experienced The Voice maybe half a dozen times in my life.

When I about thirteen we had a night I shall never forget. We had a very powerful sitting where we were prepared first by Mam and then, when she had gone deeply into her trance, our Spirit friend Miss Johnson came and prepared us even further. She told us what to do and when to stand up in a circle. It felt as though we had a myriad of Spirit friends joining us in this sacred service. We were all in an altered state of being.

The Voice arrived and we were surrounded by his love and compassion. Touching each one of us on the forehead, he gave us each a blessing, a gift of Spirit and a colour.

My blessing was 'Healing of Minds' and the colour blue. He said the healing of minds is essential now and he asked that I should sit and send out healing from my mind to the minds of sick people.

'It does not need the laying of hands,' he said. 'There is much to do in such a short time.'

In our heightened state, anything seemed possible and we knew everything we'd heard in the room that night was the truth.

I must have been around fourteen when I learned something that has stuck with me vividly down the years. During one sitting, Spirit talked about Atlantis, the mythical lost civilisation first written about by Plato in 360BC, of which our family knew nothing at the time. There have been debates from antiquity right through to modern history about its existence, with some historians claiming that it is just an allegory while others insist that there is sufficient geographical evidence to sustain the theory that its existence was fact. Argument rages over whether it was situated in the Mediterranean or the Atlantic, which doesn't help to persuade the doubters. Spirit told us that its inhabitants were a previous incarnation of humanity that had been very highly evolved spiritually and scientifically. Unfortunately they had misused their power and nearly destroyed the world. We were told that some of these people had gone to another planet and would return when the time was right. We were still being encouraged to keep faith in The Work and in ourselves and to know that it wouldn't be long before we would come into our own and know what we had to do.

Unsurprisingly, with all the upheaval I had experienced in my personal life and my own lack of natural academic talent, I left school without any qualifications and applied for a couple of shop jobs. I ended up in Brown's Trimmings, a Dickensian-looking haberdashery shop with rows and rows of floor-to-ceiling glass drawers filled with every colour and size of button, sequins and lace. We had to learn off by heart where everything was and were expected to know immediately where to find a match for the single buttons people would bring in. The shop assistants stood behind the counter with its fixed tape measure, ready to measure the yards of trimmings of every design and colour, while the owner sat above, keeping an eye on us. I will always remember the sucking noise as we put the money into a small metal pod, stuck it into the vacuumed tube and sent it off along a pulley above our heads to Mrs Brown. The owner would then check the money and receipt and send the change back down for the customer. Twenty-seven years later, when I was by now a qualified social worker, I was asked by one of my new colleagues where my first job was. Telling her it was Brown's, she said, 'Oh, that's where I was threatened with if I didn't pull my socks up at college.'

Luckily for me, I didn't stay there long. In fact, I moved to the mill where my mum worked, as it was twice the money I had been earning at Brown's I made the move primarily because I had been offered a place to train as a SRN nurse and I thought it better to earn extra cash before I took up my studies.

I had long harboured fantasies of becoming a teacher since primary school days when I had been put in charge of the younger pupils, but I believed that that would never happen to someone like me. But I did want to have a caring career, and nursing and healing was in my family. I was invited to attend in the morning for an entrance exam at Townleys General Hospital. The interview was held in a large room with me at one end of a huge polished table facing two women and a man. I can still remember some of the daft things I said in response to their questions, but they must have seen some potential and I was successful for entrance the following year on the proviso that I took a couple of O Levels.

Once settled on this course of action, I didn't mind working temporarily in the mill, even though it was seen as a step down from shop work. The mill girls were so generous and caring and they would do anything for anyone. They worked really hard as they were on piece work, but they were great storytellers and in the breaks we laughed a lot, usually about their husbands. We each had a frame of about forty cones, twenty on either side, and we had to transfer the smaller shuttles of cotton that had already gone through the process by the weavers and the spinners. If the cotton was too coarse it would break. Then using a device strapped on to our right hand we would get rid of the knots, repair it, and set it going again. It was like keeping plates spinning in the air, and we would run around re-knotting and setting down to keep the system going. The greatest satisfaction was when they were all up and running and you had a minute to stand still.

I started work at seven thirty in the morning and had to be on the bus by seven to make it in time. I worked until half past five and was always shattered at the end of the day. Like most teenagers I needed a lot of sleep. My mum said that being a winder was a step up from being a spinner which is what she did, and being a spinner was a step up from weaving. Even within the mill, the hierarchy was in place!

One night just before my seventeenth birthday, my cousin Martha, Mam, Stanley and I went to a pub in Bolton. We got talking to two chaps, one of whom, Pete, was working in the area but was originally from Yorkshire. His pal, James, had been studying for an extra year at Manchester University as part of his teacher training. James was good fun, interesting and jolly. He was nine years older than me but I was quite taken.

They were all keen golfers and we arranged to meet up for a game of golf. Even though I was useless I tagged along. James walked me home and afterwards we went out a couple of times. He'd finished his course by this time and shortly afterwards went back to Yorkshire, but we began writing to each other and he would come and visit me at weekends. It wasn't long before I fell completely in love with him. In fact I was so besotted with James at this time that during my lunch hour at the mill I would make the twenty-minute bus journey back home just to see if there was a letter from him waiting for me.

Eventually the momentous weekend arrived when I was to get on the train to Hull to see James. It sounds silly, but I had never been anywhere on my own before. Mam helped me to get ready, made sure I was looking smart and took me to the station in Manchester to put me on my train. The pair of us were nearly in tears, even though I was only going away overnight!

Arriving in Hull I discovered that James' family was far posher than ours. They had serviettes! Even though James' mum was a Yorkshire woman, she was quite middle class, having been brought up on her father's farm. She couldn't bring herself to say the word 'mill' and instead would ask me what time I had left the office. But she was very kind and welcoming and a wonderful cook too. She made the best Yorkshire curd cheesecake I have ever tasted.

James and I quickly became very serious about each other and, even though I had planned to start my nursing course in Bolton, we decided to get married. So the nursing course went down the tubes and, although I intended to take it up in Yorkshire, I never did.

I was married three weeks before my eighteenth birthday and I cried all the way to my honeymoon, knowing I was leaving not just my home but, crucially, my mother behind. It must have been great for James' ego! Nonetheless, James and I got a flat and settled in to married life. I took a job in a very smart shoe shop, a place with boxes of shoes from floor to ceiling accessed only by climbing great high ladders.

I stopped work when my first child, Stephen, was born in 1968, followed by my daughter Joanne two years later. Although I was young and clueless and found the lack of sleep and worry about Stephen's colic really hard, I loved motherhood. Like most young mothers all my conversations were about the babies and what they had done. I was totally preoccupied.

James applied for a more prestigious teaching post down south and I had to relocate two hundred miles away with two children under three, moving even further away from my beloved mother and family in the North. The separation from my mother was particularly hard to bear. I had always been so close and dependent on her. I missed her terribly when my married life began and this state of affairs didn't improve with time. Everything changed so quickly in those few short years; I went from being a teenager at home with her mam to a bride, and then by the age of twenty-two I became a mother myself to my two children – a long, long way from home to boot. I emerged from being a highly dependent daughter to a mother, with not much in the way of life experience in between.

I was young and unsophisticated and my problems were compounded by having married a man nine years my senior. I was immature and over time we became estranged, neither able to meet the other's needs. I had married too young and too quickly and although I will always love James for giving me my two beautiful children, it was clear that the marriage was not going to survive. The crunch point came when James was offered another job, involving another big move, and I decided not to join him.

So by the age of twenty-five I was divorced. I made the decision to stay put rather than return up North because I had a job I wanted to do, a reasonable wage and, more importantly, I could have the school holidays off to be with my own children. By this time I was working as a nursery nurse in a special unit attached to a mainstream school, helping to care for what in those days were referred to as 'maladjusted children'.

In modern parlance they would be called children with special needs, but whatever their label there were a lot of behavioural difficulties among them, which gave rise to stress and high sickness rates among staff. Because of the absenteeism, supply staff would be brought in and this constant cycle of change was exhausting and certainly no good for the children.

Even though I had a good heart and loved the kids, I was completely unqualified and often would be left for days to cope with a class full of them on my own. They would all run rings around me.

It was a demanding job, but given the financial strain I was under after parting from James, I could hardly chuck it in. Despite the pressures, it was for me the fulfilment of an earlier dream, and very soon a new head teacher arrived and matters improved. Shortly after her appointment we were all moved to a specially built unit attached to a junior school. There was a family atmosphere at this school and I began to love my work with the children.

My new boss was fantastically supportive and her accommodating attitude made my working life possible. The other staff were very understanding when my own children were sick or I was other-wise indisposed. James continued to be a doting father and would come down every weekend to visit the children. In the beginning when he'd left we hadn't told the children we were separating, just that Dad had another job and would come home at weekends. We continued to go out as a family on these visits and present a united front.

About a year after James's move we told them that we were in fact splitting up. They managed to take it in their stride, having grown accustomed to not seeing Dad during the week. Whatever other mistakes I have made in my life I feel proud of the way that James and I handled our parting with regard to the children. We never involved them in our disagreements or had anything negative to say about the other in their presence, which is, I believe, as it should be. As they grew older, I would put the children on the train at my end and James would pick them up at his.

The years that followed our separation were an incredible struggle, and having to take financial responsibility for myself and the children was a terrifying prospect. At the age of twenty-five, I had never had a bank account or signed a cheque, and had no idea of how such matters were conducted. James had always taken care of everything and given me housekeeping money for food and things for the children. Not knowing how to go about taking charge of my financial affairs I went to our local branch of Barclays Bank and asked to see somebody. I was given an appointment and met with a lovely, fatherly man in his mid-fifties who set aside a couple of hours for me. Seeing my help-lessness in the face of managing money, he very patiently took me through my incomings and outgoings and showed me how to balance the books. Having listed everything, he advised me to set up standing orders so that I wouldn't have to worry about getting bills paid on time. He even showed me how to write a cheque.

He performed this great kindness not knowing just how helpful he had been to me and if there is one person I will seek out when I pass over to the other world it will be him, so that I can thank him for what he did. He gave me so much independence and empowered me to get on with my life in those two short hours.

But it was not just financially that I was feeling the strain. Emotionally, I felt vulnerable and scared. I hated sleeping alone. Before my divorce I had no experience of independence whatsoever and now I was lonely and had very little in the way of a social life.

I did have a babysitter who would come and mind the children once a week so that I could go and play badminton. It was here that I met and started an affair with an older married man with children. It was not an ideal relationship but it offered something in the way of stability and support and I was grateful for what little comfort I could get. I would never have asked him to leave his wife for me. I justified my actions by thinking that I was the one who was sacrificing and being hurt because I didn't want to break up his family. I am wiser and less selfish now and I regret the hurt we caused. The relationship lasted several years and helped to ease the feelings of loneliness and vulnerability, so I will always be grateful to him for that.

Other relationships followed, but none could give me the love I sought. I wanted to feel special and to experience the glow of courtship and romance that I had missed out on, having married so young. My expectations were perhaps unrealistic.

I have a very clear memory of this time that was one of acute embarrassment. Those are usually the incidents you remember most clearly – the lovely ones *and* the embarrassing ones. I continued to play a lot of badminton, and one evening the fixture secretary, a retired major, called round. We had just settled down with a cup of tea at the round dining table when my son, Stephen, who was about ten, came in and made some mildly cheeky remark. Normally I would have let this go, but I felt I had to behave with some authority in front of the major. I stood up and told Stephen off. He just laughed and, waving his hands about, asked me what I was going to do about it. As soon as I stood up and started chasing him around the table, I knew I had made the wrong decision. Every time I caught up with him, Stephen would change direction and laugh. The Major's face was a picture. Eventually I gave in and sat down red-faced and panting. Raising my eyebrow I said 'Kids! Now Major, which team are we playing?'

Still troubled by my lack of success at school, I

started to study for a couple of O Levels by correspondence course. I would get the kids to bed and work on my English Language and Literature and Maths. I would do the work, send it off and wait eagerly for the reply. It was a thrill to receive the feedback and for the first time I was being complimented on my ideas and hard work. This was when I first came across the work of William Blake and began an immediate and lifelong love affair with his ideas and philosophy. Blake's sense of the divine, and the spirit that infused his poetry, especially *Songs of Innocence and Experience*, struck a deep chord within me. I was no great scholar and managed only a C in English and a D in Maths, but I was thrilled.

My mam would come down and see me sometimes, and we would occasionally have a sitting when the children had gone to bed. The Doctor's son, Stephen, was most often the Spirit who would come through. I always felt a special relationship with him. He told me he worked with certain people here on earth influencing The Work and that he would be coming back permanently in a new incarnation. He said that we would meet up in the future to further The Work, and that I would know him when I saw him. Not all Spirits had to reincarnate as a child – they could come back for brief periods to influence important events. Stephen was always very kind and understanding, and helped me get through the dark times. He always talked about keeping faith as though it was essential for The Work to be successful.

Maybe I was missing the contact with Spirit that being at home in Horwich provided or maybe I was becoming prey to strange fears, but in 1975, when I was twenty-seven, I started to have a strange foreboding that I was going to die at the age of thirty-five. It wasn't a particularly tormenting fear, in the sense that it wasn't on my mind constantly, but from time to time I just had this sense that I was going to die. I didn't feel terror or indeed anything much except acceptance.

In fact it felt as if there was no let-up in the relentless pressure on me, a young single mother struggling to work and make ends meet. Although the children and I were fortunate to live in a nice new house that James and I had bought, I was desperately lonely and craved a happy marriage.

By and large I have been blessed with an optimistic temperament, but there was one weekend when the loneliness became unbearable. The children had gone on holiday with their dad and I felt empty and hopeless. Like most mothers I was looking forward to having a breather from the children only to miss them horribly once they had gone. As much as I enjoyed the break from responsibility, the time alone left me pondering the mess of my life. It is not in my nature to have ever contemplated suicide, but on this particular night everything seemed to come crashing down. It was towards the end of my relationship with the married man and I was very, very low, more desperate than I have ever felt before or since.

But I had never lost my faith in Spirit and I always prayed. That night I prayed with all my heart for help. I went to bed feeling completely beaten, little knowing that I was about to have an experience that has remained with me to this day, such was its beauty, radiance and clarity. It was all the more remarkable for the fact that it rose out of the ashes of utter dejection.

I lay in bed, swamped in feelings of loss and failure. As I lay there feeling empty and hollow, I had the sensation of slowly receding into my own body as if I was gradually sinking. I couldn't fight it or resist this perception. I just sank further and further down. I was not asleep but neither was I particularly aware of being on the bed. I was conscious only of travelling downwards in utter darkness and despair for what seemed like an age, aware not just of my own but of other people's pain too.

Just as I thought I could no longer tolerate the feelings of nausea and physical and emotional anguish any longer, I started to feel a change – a strange sensation of rising on a slight incline, very, very slowly. As this upward movement progressed, I started to feel lighter and less ill. I then noticed the tiniest pinprick of light in the far distance, which was pulling me in like a magnet. As I was drawn nearer to the dot of brightening light, my perception was of travelling along a tunnel. I began to shed the feeling of loss and pain and a new feeling of peace of mind began to take its place. This was entirely new to me. I had never experienced serenity or the lack of worry, anxiety, loss or hurt. But this was love like I had never experienced, completely off the scale. It totally enveloped me. I felt a tremendous healing take place, the rays of light that were bathing me pulling me deeper into this ever-increasing circle of light, creating a sense of excitement and, moreover, the certainty that I was going home.

The light enveloped me, but more than that, it *was* me. I WAS LIGHT! The closest feeling to this I had felt on earth was the love I felt for my children, but even that paled in comparison. Over the years I have struggled to find the words to explain this experience to others – but how can I describe the indescribable? The best I can manage is that it was the most exquisite feeling of love I have ever felt. Even today, some thirty years later, I am moved to tears when I reconnect to that experience. It was to change my whole outlook on life.

For the first time ever, I did not need anyone else to make me feel loved or alive, or to give me an identity. I was just it, the thing in itself, I was LOVE. It was a self-replenishing love that had no need to give or receive in order to give me purpose or make me feel worthy in the act of loving another. On the contrary, I felt quite self-*less*; I was at one and connected to everything and everyone. I was not separate from love nor always trying to possess it, I *was* it, I was complete, I was pure love. Way beyond anything I had ever felt in my life before, this sensation completely enveloped me and relieved the pain I had been carrying for years. I had never lost my faith in Spirit and I had always prayed, but it was usually for what I wanted and what I needed. This was to prove the turning point. When I pray now it is to offer thanks.

In absolute peace for the first time in my life, I did not want to return from this place. I had let go of 'me' and was suspended in peace. Just as I was basking in this place of serenity and love, a giant of a man appeared in shining white robes before me. The sensations I felt both for and from this man were overwhelming. I felt at one with this soul, with whom I shared an extraordinary level of love and awareness. Although he did not speak, I felt his compassion and love for me as he pointed his finger back for me to return – it was not my time. In an instant I was back on my bed and I cried. I no longer just believed in the existence of God anymore, I *knew* God. What is more, I knew that I could heal. What The Voice had revealed to me earlier back in Bolton was now confirmed. My destiny was to heal others, as I had been healed myself.

When I woke up after this experience I felt almost

as if I had died. I felt unwell for some time but gradually the most profound change began to stir within me. This life-changing moment was to be the turning point, and from that moment I could no longer resist the urge to return to my roots and family.

Coming up to Christmas that year, I had taken some extra work in a hotel to make ends meet. There I met Mike, who ripped through my life like a tornado. Good-looking, with dark hair and twinkly eyes, Mike was funny, charming and had the ability to make me feel very special. I was going through a profound personal transformation after my experience in the tunnel and Mike gave me confidence to follow my heart. In return, I provided him with the stability he needed.

He moved in with me and it wasn't long before his daughter, who was living with a previous girl-friend of Mike's, came to live with us also. The children all got on well and Mike's daughter was lovely. My two children and I had been on our own for years and when I think back now I realise how welcoming, selfless, and understanding my children were in accepting such a big change, purely because they wanted me to be happy.

Mike was a man who would follow his spirit of adventure fearlessly and, unlike me, change came easily to him. When I told him of my wishes to move back up North, he gave me the courage to follow my dream. He too was looking for a new start in a new place.

Soon I was leaving some wonderful friends and a job I loved, but the energy of change would brook no opposition. I was certain that I was being guided and led back, not just by Mike but by Spirit too. I took that leap of faith, despite the protests from my children who were settled in schools with all their friends around them. I was being propelled forwards by an unseen force and the momentum of starting over and the need for renewal was irresistible. As if to underline the rightness of this decision, my house sold quickly and in 1983, after seventeen years of living away from the place I would always think of as home, I returned to Horwich.

Delighted to have us back, my mam and stepdad accommodated the four of us in their tiny two-bedroomed flat for a couple of months. My poor son slept on a mattress in a cupboard long before Harry Potter made it fashionable!

In due course we found a nice house not far from Hope Street in view of the Pike. From there we enjoyed walks up Rivington again and started going back to the Spiritualist Church. It was a special time and the children were happy at their new school. Mike was instrumental not only in giving me the courage and the support to move, but he was also responsible for getting me back in touch with my natural dad and I am eternally grateful to him for that.

I remember the day so clearly. The children were

in school and Mike casually asked about my birth father. As I started to tell Mike about him, I couldn't contain the pent-up feelings of loss from two decades without my dad in my life. I had buried twenty years of suppressed emotion about my dad and though I heard about him and his life through my brother, who had maintained a close relationship, I had not been in touch with him myself. I don't know how long I cried or what memories came up but it was clear that I still felt a great deal of pain about being apart from him.

I had stopped seeing my dad as a child because I found it so difficult, but Mike, who had sons he didn't see as often as he wanted, understood the pain from the other side. After hearing the story, true to his style, Mike said 'Right, get in touch now!' and insisted he take me down to see him. We went, and I resumed my relationship with my father and also got to know his children from his second marriage, my half-brothers and sisters. It was a wonderful reunion that would bridge the gap of our time apart.

For the last twenty years of my father's life he came to stay with me regularly and we were reunited in love and laughter again, as close as we had been in the early years. By this time, Mam and I were having regular circles on our own again, perhaps every couple of months, either at my home or Mam's. To my great joy, Dad joined in the re-formed circles and participated in this lovely relationship between the two worlds as though there had been no gap.

There was no bitterness I could discern between Mam and Dad. On my father's visits, my dad and my stepdad Stanley – who had known each other for years – would revisit their old haunts, having a pint and reminiscing. No matter what had happened on a personal level, everyone's faith in Spirit never wavered. Although Stan had never got over his divorce and the loss of his own children, he looked after us all and put up with my Grandma living with him for twenty years.

In retrospect, I see that another part of Dad's life purpose was to initiate and support the circles with my mam. He was perfect for this job because of his inquiring and discerning mind and his positive outlook. Together they created a happy and joyful environment in which the Spirit friends could come through and leave the message for humanity to be shared long after their passing. He had great faith in my mam's mediumship and they shared a love and respect for each other throughout their lives.

The fact that Mike was a go-getter meant that, despite the uncertainty, great things were possible for me at this time. The reunion with my father was a joyful affair and over the next twenty years my dad came to stay with me lots of times. Every morning during these visits he would go for his *Daily Mirror*, study the form then go and put his bet on. I became very familiar with betting fore-casts. Most days he would lose but, with the eternal optimism of the gambler, tomorrow was always another day.

We would laugh and reminisce about the old times, remembering his funny stories from his time in the erecting shop at the loco works, and discussing what we had learned at the sittings. My Dad never lost faith in the Spirit friends and The Work despite all his years away. The friends, for their part, were delighted to see us all together again. Around this time Dad's brother, Uncle Fred, and his wife, Auntie Bella, rejoined the sittings. They would hold them at their house every week, providing lovely food, home-brew and a good sing-song to follow. Afterwards, my two dads would go out for a drink together and they resumed a child-hood friendship and the Spirit relationship that had kept them united through thick and thin. My brother, Dad and me would go up Rivi again to all the old haunts and it was as if we had never been apart.

Funnily enough, given my dad's ever-present need for 'proof', it was when we had restarted these sittings with him that I saw my mam disappear in front of my own eyes during two separate occa-sions, once at Uncle Fred's and once at our house. It was a remarkable experience and I could not stop blinking. Later, when we discussed it, I thought perhaps it might be an optical illusion. I will always look for the material explanation first, though in this case none was forthcoming. Mam suggested that I was 'seeing' beyond this physical world where her material body did not exist.

I can also vividly recall that on one occasion, on my son Stephen's birthday when we were back in Horwich, we could smell candle smoke as if somebody had just blown out the candles on a cake, almost as if Spirit was sending us a celebratory message. Stephen smelled it too. I know that in the telling it sounds like magic and totally unreal, but to us it was real and matter-of-fact.

For what it's worth, the physical 'proofs' that I and others witnessed hold the least interest for me – I always believe that it is the spiritual message of the sittings that is significant. Working on ourselves to uncover Spirit is the key: we ourselves are the proof! But my father was always interested in physical materialisations.

Having Dad around brought everything alive again and it was joyful being with him. If something spiritual was going on in the area and my stepdad didn't want to come, I would take Mam and Dad. One of the first Mind, Body and Spirit events was held in a Manchester hotel about twenty-five years ago and I took them both. When we got there Ray Gosling was filming it. My mam spent the whole time ducking down every time the camera came near in case the people of Horwich thought something was going on with her ex-husband!

But despite the gratitude I felt towards Mike for getting me home and back in touch with my dad, our relationship did not continue to run smoothly. After a while Mike was travelling again with his job and he met someone who suited him better than me. It was a difficult time for everyone but I now see that we came together for a reason, to act as catalysts for each other and bring about the change we both needed. Mike's daughter stayed a little while but was eventually reunited with her brothers and mother. Although sadly my relationship could not be sustained with Mike, we brought spiritual gifts to each other that changed us for the better and I shall always be grateful and remember the good times.

Once Mike had gone, the way was clear for Mam and I to begin our spiritual path hand in hand once more, and I started to feel as though I had come back in more ways than one. I was free from a relationship for the first time in my adult life and it was a revelation. It was so liberating and wonderful to realise I could come into my own, now that I didn't need to pour all my creativity and energies into thoughts of men and romantic notions. It was to be an intense period of spiritual development for me and Mam, and we spent hours and hours talking. We spent more time on meditation, moving into spiritual self-development. Mam also helped me to nurture my sensitivity to Spirit, experimenting with psychometry to see if I could receive.

Mam had always told me that I was too material, not in the sense of craving possessions but in terms of being grounded and earthbound and possibly too sceptical. Where others might be more credulous and believing, I never swallowed anything whole, sticking with my own inner knowing. If Spirit came through with messages that didn't ring true to me, I simply wouldn't accept that they had anything to teach me. Mam knew that in order for me to develop spiritually I had to feed my faith. She encouraged me to seek outlets for this development.

When I'd arrived back in Horwich from the South in 1983, I found that Mam had gone back to the Spiritualist Church where Mrs Sherrington, known to us as Auntie Lily, was president. Following in Mam's footsteps, I too rejoined the Church after a gap of nearly twenty-five years. It was so good to come home to that welcoming building with its beautiful angel banner hanging on the wall behind the rostrum. Desperate to make up for lost time, I attended every service and helped with every event.

So, now in my thirties, I started attending the clairvoyant services again. I loved the singing and the Divine Service where the medium expounds philosophy on a Sunday. That was the best part for me. I had returned to the powerful and dynamic spiritual environment that my soul had been crying out for during all those years down south.

I began to appreciate how progressive the Spiritualist Church had always been. The healing services were a direct precursor to the now widespread New Age concept of healing, and the Church had been able to provide this as well as comfort, education, friendship and communion with Spirit for those who are bereaved, ill and searching. The Church still attracts generous souls who work tirelessly to provide a place of worship and awakening. Through its open-arm policy of inclusivity it has acted as a springboard for generations of otherwise disenfranchised people on their spiritual journeys. The forerunner of the whole Mind, Body and Spirit philosophy, Spiritualism offers a beautiful, dogma-free template for a life of peace and serenity. Of course it does not prevent life's vicissitudes from coming to your door, but it gives you a wonderful set of principles with which to deal with them. I owe it so much.

I have never claimed to be a medium or felt moved to develop that side of myself, not really needing to with Mam around, but I had always been interested and felt drawn to healing. It seemed a natural progression to join the Healing Group in the Spiritualist Church. Healing is sometimes misunderstood, and the impression often nurtured by the unscrupulous is that of a human being with special powers who can cure the sick. There are always charlatans who prey on the vulnerable in this way but genuine healers do not claim to be gifted with any special powers, we are merely channels for Spirit to work through. We don't *do* the healing, we *allow* it. There are hundreds of wonderful men and women who work in this way, totally free of charge, up and down the country in complete anonymity. But Harry Edwards was probably the most famous healer Britain has ever known.

Harry Edwards started his career in printing but was increasingly drawn into the healing profession after a medium told him he was an instrument for spiritual healing. Feeling compelled to take this path, his healing work grew quickly. Word spread of the remarkable healings that had been channeled through him by the Divine Spirit. Harry Edwards dedicated his life to spreading the word about the Spirit world's ministry and commitment to working with us as teachers and healers. In 1950 he fought to overturn the law that prevented registered healers from practising in hospital alongside conventional medics. He founded the Federation of Spiritual Healers in 1955 and was a teacher and an author.

His main work, however, was in the countless thousands of one-to-one healings he performed. Harry Edwards filled halls all over the country and had doctors witnessing the miracles in order to legitimise spiritual healing. When he died in 1976, he gifted his home, the Healing Sanctuary, Burrows Lea Country House in Guilford, Surrey, to continue as a charitable Trust, offering healing and sanctuary.

His pioneering work had inspired many people to train as healers and has led to a worldwide acceptance of spiritual healing and a resurgence of ancient practices such as acupuncture and Reiki. As I was writing this I received an overwhelming sense of love from Harry and I know that he continues serving humanity from the Light.

Becoming a healer involves on-the-job training. Although theoretically open to all, it is a painstaking and exhaustive process, involving hundreds of hours of observations, giving and receiving healing, and continual tests.

At the healing services we would begin with a healing prayer and the atmosphere was very sacred and calm. The healers would stand behind their chairs and people could choose to whom they wanted to go. My main aim during these hour-long services was to get myself out of the way and let the healing come through. I usually knew when it was working as I felt a wonderful thrill going through my body to the tips of my fingers, and I would feel guided to lay my hands on a certain part of the body. There would be healing of specific physical pain and also general healing where people would just want to feel the comforting touch of another human being, especially the elderly who often lived very isolated, lonely lives. To watch healing occur is miraculous and moving and over the years I saw countless people relieved of both their physical and emotional pain.

These early years after my return to Horwich were an intense and lovely time for me and Mam, perhaps the most precious of my life. Mam and I healed each other and others from our past through prayer, meditation and communication with Spirit. Having kept a little bit of money back from the sale of the house down South, I was free to concentrate on meditation and The Work and what was to come without the distraction of having to find a job. Mam would tell me of the infinite opportunities spirit people would have to learn and experience things they had desired to do on earth but for whatever reason had not. These could be in the creative arts – music, writing or painting – or gardening, sailing, dance, being with children or animals or whatever they wished or needed. Restrictions of opportunity, time, money or disabilities did not exist in the Spirit World.

There was also the opportunity to experience parenthood if this had been hoped for but denied to them on earth. There would be training for this, but once evolved the spirits would become guardians in the children's realm. Children would have the most wonderful, joyful experiences growing up in the Spirit World. They would always remain attached to, and often work as guides influencing their earth parents. Love can never be extinguished. If it had been a difficult relationship on earth the children would receive understanding and project healing to their parents. A profession could be studied and trained for. Training to be a Spirit guide or learning new life skills for the next life or simply reading in the libraries were all on offer. In fact, whatever was your idea of Heaven could be yours! Of course that might also include earthly addictions to food, drink, sex, drugs, unhealthy emotions and even dogmatic belief! There were lots of communities continuing these life styles, but with help from Angels, these needs would become less and less as the love and light healed. The permanent energies of the spiritual would eventually replace the short term emotional 'high' received from substitutes. Spirits progressed through the Realms as their thought patterns changed. There were seven realms of understanding, but they were invisible until the time when a person was ready to move on to another realm of understanding and perception.

In other words, when an individual became weary or found less nourishment and felt less enthusiasm for their present ideas, perceptions would change, and gradually subtle changes would take place in themselves and their environment. They would meet new friends and be drawn to new interests. The old realm of understanding would fade from view and they would start to perceive and express themselves on a new and more vibrant dimension of beauty, light and colour. This higher frequency Realm would be their new Heaven until they were ready to move on again.

Mam explained how people build their Spirit homes and environments through deeds and actions performed whilst on earth and that we could visit the Spirit World in our dream state to meet up with our loved ones, and even attend spiritual meetings. This was called Astral Travelling.

Everything was thought form in the Spirit world. The musical concerts would be heard, felt, sensed and seen in sound waves of colour and movement! The Spirit friends would think of being with someone or going somewhere here or in heaven and be there in an instant as if they were being magnetically drawn to their desires.

Rescue work would always be done in groups of Spirits whose intention was to help those in the dark by taking love and light to the lower realms. The group intention had to be held at all times by the rescuer workers and they had to be highly trained not to let their compassion allow in any of the negative thoughts of those they were trying to help. Thoughts are powerful living things! When these troubled souls formed the intention to move on from their negativity, they would see the light, and their thought patterns and perceptions would change, making the rescue possible. Again, when they were ready a new higher realm of understanding would become visible, as the old one disappeared. We were told that everyone on Earth has a guide but that some people are so enveloped in negativity that it is difficult for this guide to get through. Help, however, is always there if asked for. The moment a request for help is sent the Angels are there. We also had sittings when the Spirit friends reiterated everything we had been told years before but this time we were being guided to find out things for ourselves rather than rely upon them to tell us everything. They asked us to be patient and to be prepared for something new they were planning to bring into our lives. As they had told us in the early days, we would meet new people and know them by the strong bond we felt. Of course I had met people throughout my life who I knew to be kindred spirits, but this time they said we would meet more and more to further The Work.

Then within a year it happened. Now I knew why Spirit intended me to return to Horwich at this time. Mam had taken a trip to Ireland to visit relatives and she was standing by Lake Lough Leane in the west of Ireland when she heard The Voice say, 'You are to start the Rainbow Group.'

Never one to doubt the instructions of the Spirit friends, Mam returned home to tell me the new plan, and in 1984 the Rainbow Group was formed, much to our excitement. Soon after her Irish revelation she received further instruction.

'It is time to take your mediumship to a second phase and to show others how to receive and transmit from our world. This group you shall call the Rainbow Group shall spread out in the world. We shall tell you how to run these evenings and, as before in your previous circle, we shall send you, the people, to pioneer this new way of working.'

Eire had always featured highly in Spirit messages and in the early years my Mum was told that The Work would start its final manifestation in this lovely land, as well as in the high mountains around the world. The South American country of Peru featured prominently in my Mam's mind too, and from the early sixties Mam would often talk about it and say how much she wanted to visit there. She had a profound spiritual connection to these two countries. She said that Spirit beings would appear from these high and spiritual places on earth. They would come down from the mountains but only when the time was right.

When she told me this I felt a huge thrill going through my body. In my mind's eye I saw all these radiant beings clothed in vibrant colours coming down the mountains to greet us.

The Spirit friends kept their word and many new kindred souls entered our lives. One of them was Dorothy. Tall, slim and elegant with long auburn hair, she wore long skirts and floaty dresses, a great sixties look that suited her height. She had done years of yoga and spiritual work and became central to the Rainbow meetings. We are still great friends today.

Spirit told my mam how to run the evenings and

we were very excited on the first Friday night of the Rainbow Group. At the end of that first evening when everyone had left, I remember laughing with my mam and Dorothy about how she had presented us with the inspiration at the beginning of the meeting. With her captive audience of about twenty spiritual seekers, Mam introduced the first Rainbow meeting with: 'There will be no bosses,' and went on to say, '. . . and now I shall tell you what to do!' In her enthusiasm to let everyone know what the Spirit world had told her about the Rainbow nights being a democratic arena with no particular leader, she had laid down the law like a seasoned tyrant! Mam was always ready to laugh at herself, repeating it to us time and time again till we laughed so much we were hurting.

Of course, what she was trying to get across was the fact that everyone would be equal and would be encouraged to channel their own inspiration and truths rather than it coming from just one person, a medium like herself. We were all being trained to receive and awaken to our own power and divinity.

It was to be the start of an amazing and truly inspirational time in our lives. The Rainbow Group ran every week for twelve years until my Mum died, and it has continued on and off ever since. During that period over a hundred different people have been members, with some attending for short periods before they moved on and others who have stayed in contact for years. The evenings encouraged spirituality in a wonderful way and had the same joyful energy of the first sittings. We met every Friday night and each member, if they wished, would devise a creative evening around the arts, Spirit, angels, meditation, religions, music, self-development, dance and looking at mandalas (sacred Hindu or Buddhist art). In fact, anything creative that was fun and generated laughter, fulfillment and spiritual development. The inspiration from Spirit and from each other was astonishing and everyone blossomed in confidence and self-esteem, realising how much knowledge and inspiration they had to give and receive, regardless of social circumstances or education. We all hailed from very ordinary backgrounds but the Rainbow Group made us feel we had something unique and special to offer. This was long before Mind, Body and Spirit workshops and spiritual retreats had become commonplace. In between the Fridays our week was filled with ideas and inspiration for the next group and we would have to keep a pad and paper with us at all times to be prepared for inspiration. Most Rainbow Group members have continued on their spiritual path in their working life, turning an inspiration into a vocation.

We each took it in turns to run the nights and would spend a lot of time researching or just 'receiving' for our night's presentation. The evening would always start with a prayer and a meditation, sometimes silent and sometimes guided or with music. The focus was often on learning about different religions, finding out what we had in common rather than what separated us. We would research songs, chants or dances from other religious practices or ceremonies and enact them ourselves, teaching us to respect other cultures and broaden our outlooks and knowledge.

Other nights we would make a sand picture or colour a mandala. We might listen to a piece of music that would move us beyond words, or do divination using the *I Ching* or Chinese astrology. We would take turns drawing each other's auras, feeling them intuitively even if we couldn't see them. It was amazing how similar the colours and shapes and our interpretations would be. Sometimes we would use 'angel cards' to help us reflect on the gifts we may bring to the world. Other nights we would simply have fun, singing, dancing and doing drama improvisation. Laughter and joy was always at the forefront of our Spirit messages; they always encouraged us to be happy as it was the best vibration for our Spirit guides and angels to draw close and make their presence felt.

One weekend we had a wonderful workshop called 'God's Child' devised by Clive Koerner. We each entered the sacred circle and met our 'spiritual elders'. We would ask what might be holding us back from finding the love within, and we would receive counsel on our path. We took on the roles of both the seekers and the wise elders that weekend.

Many nights like these encouraged our higher selves to emerge and to see ourselves in a new light. We could be open and reveal ourselves in all our guises. We learned to trust and to recognise that everyone has the same problems, and to let go of negative patterns that may have been passed down for generations. We had to stop worrying about being judged, to let go of shame and prejudice, and in doing so to forgive both ourselves and other people. We were learning to be sensitive and find peace, to see ourselves as Spirits who were having a human experience. This allowed us to go beyond our earthly personality and let the Spirit mind come to the fore. Without realising it, we were looking at ourselves as multi-dimensional beings who could choose to respond in new ways rather than being purely reactive.

It was to be a time of new departures for me in so many ways. The conviction I had had of my physical death at the age of thirty-five was proved false, but it was the death of the part of me that was full of need. It was at thirty-five that I lost a sense of emotional neediness and was able to be on my own for the first time ever. This time turned out to be a massive turning point for me.

With no man around, I was able to think really clearly about what I wanted to do. I had loved the teaching I had done in my previous job and I now looked into doing teacher training. This involved first getting a degree. I dithered about for a while and in 1984, at thirty-six years of age, I applied to study for a degree in Philosophy at the Bolton College of Further Education. I was interviewed by a very sympathetic and kind History tutor, who thought I would probably make a good candidate. However, as a mature student without the usual qualifications I would have to submit an essay for assessment. I chose to write about George Orwell's *1984*. I had never got on that well at school but my brother Thomas and ex-husband James were wonderful in helping me put my application together and overcome my lack of confidence. There was, too, something bullish about me at that time and my perseverance and refusal to accept that I wasn't clever enough paid off. I have no doubt that Spirit was leading me all the way. My essay was accepted.

That summer of 1985 before I started at Bolton was a wonderful period. The children were busy out making new friends and I was spending a lot of time with my mam, talking about the family and our links to Spirit. It was round this time that I got back in touch with my cousin Martha (John and Edith's daughter, from the original circle) and sometimes she would come over and the three of us would all go out together. We used to go off and explore all sorts of places and ideas that caught our fancy, usually something with a spiritual angle.

It was Martha who first told us about the

Swedenborg College in Bury, where novice minis-
ters to the New Church were trained. She had heard
that they were having an evening talk by one of
their number, a Rev Michael Stanley, so we decided
to go. Dr Stanley had been following a successful
career in America as a physicist, when he experienced a calling to the Church. Heeding the call, he
gave up his scientific career and came to England to
train as a minister in the New Church. He is such a
charismatic man and the talk was very inspirational.

At the end of his talk, he announced that he
would be holding a weekend workshop around the
teachings of Emanuel Swedenborg at the college.
That evening about seven of us including Mam
signed up to attend. I had heard and read a little
about Swedenborg, because of his influence on
William Blake, but that weekend was the first time
I really got to know and understand his philosophy.
The weekend didn't feel much like a workshop and
there was no attempt to convert us to the beliefs
of the New Church. It was more a collection of
informal discussion groups. Michael would introduce a topic and let the group steer the course of
the subsequent discussion. Despite the informality
of the weekend I nevertheless learned all about
Swedenborg's trips into the Spirit world, his
philosophy and his teachings.

What I found extraordinary was how similar his
teachings were to the message that Mam had been
telling us about all our lives. There was a real

synchronicity between their philosophies. Mam was significantly involved in these discussions and was able to contribute enormous value to the weekend. It gave me a much clearer insight into the message that my mam had been receiving and sharing with us for all those years and I was impressed to hear her speak so knowledgeably.

On the first evening, we had gathered together for our first discussion and were all sitting round chatting, when in walked a slender, upright man wearing bedroom slippers. We thought that this was a bit odd, until we learned that he was living there at the college, having met and befriended Michael Stanley at the Findhorn spiritual community in Scotland. As soon as I saw Clive, I knew immediately that here was another soulmate. The connection between us was instant and Clive felt it as well. Six feet tall and fair-haired, Clive was a very good listener, the sort of person who was very quiet until he got to know you and only then would you realise how intelligent and well-read he was. There was also an immediate bond between Clive and my cousin Martha, and in the years that followed they became very close.

Throughout the following months and years we were to attend many workshops, discussion groups and meetings at the Swedenborg College in Bury. They also held weekend retreats at the college in Purley Chase, near Birmingham, and there I learned more about the strength of the spiritual connection between us and the Spirit world. The emphasis on these retreats was not so much on channelling, spiritual manifestation and phenomenon, but more about us as eternal spirits, communing with and being guided by angels and Spirits, and the relationship we all have with our God. I found the whole experience very easy to absorb and accept. The weekends were also wonderful explorations of ourselves, our weaknesses and strengths, which we accessed through sacred chants, singing, dance and, most of all, through group discussion and sharing. We were sometimes asked to help out by doing some little jobs in the college, such as gardening or clearing up.

Meanwhile my first day at Bolton College arrived and I went down to the village to get the bus for the five-mile trip. Thinking back, I must have looked quite frumpy, plain and middle-aged, with my knee-length straight skirt, blouse and cardigan. As the bus got closer to Bolton, I remember the sense of apprehension, nervousness and excitement I was feeling. About a mile from the college, just near the student flats, the bus stopped and I heard a young man asking the conductor where to get off for Bolton College. As he came up the steps I told him I was going there and offered to show him the right stop and the way to college from there. He was a young man, about eighteen, very tall and slender with a gothic/punk look about him. His thick black hair was brushed up into standing spikes and he had a battered leather jacket on over faded, torn and scruffy jeans. A skull and cross bones ring dangled from one ear. Thanking me, he introduced himself as Paul and plonked down next to me.

I don't think we stopped talking for nearly three years. What an odd couple we must have made walking to college: the tall, skinny punk and middle-aged mumsy me. People must have mistaken us for a mother and her rebellious son.

As it turned out, we were on the same Honours degree course in Humanities. We had to choose three subjects to study in the first year, before dropping one and concentrating on the other two. We both chose History, Philosophy and English Literature. As soon as we met there was an immediate connection. Whenever things like this have happened to me, I always think back to what the Spirit friends used to say about the right people coming together at the right time, and I knew that Paul would become a very important part of my life. After the first year, during which Paul spent most of his time at our house, he came to lodge with us. Being close in age, my son Stephen and he became very good friends, and he went on to become a vital part of the Rainbow groups taking place most weekends. We became inseparable during the following three years, and he felt like a second son. We have stayed very close ever since. He is now married with two beautiful daughters and my husband and I have been privileged to become honorary grandparents.

At the end of that first year I chose Philosophy and English Literature as my subjects to continue forward. I absolutely loved being a student and everything that went with it. Not only was I being fired by wonderful concepts and philosophy, amazed that the discussion of ideas counted as work, but I got to prop up the bar at lunchtime and put the world to rights. All in all I got to experience the freedom and joy of learning that I had missed out on first time round, having married and started a family so young.

There were quite a few other mature students on my course, possibly because this was at a time when you could still get a grant just because you wanted to learn. One of us was Joe, a retired sixty-year-old with a lovely Lancashire accent. On the first day, one of our female tutors stood up to introduce herself to us all and, giving her name, asked us not to call her 'love'. Within a minute Joe quite unintentionally said, 'Excuse me, love, how do you say that fella's name, Des-car-tees?' She wasn't pleased.

It was a heady and amazing time and I made some lifelong friends, including my Philosophy tutor, a man who inspired and encouraged me. In 1988, I completed my degree with dissertations on Blake and Wordsworth and even had the nerve to write an essay on 'The Nature of God' in five thousand words.

In fact I had to call on William Blake to help me write my dissertation! Having left it all to the last minute, I was completely at the end of my tether and feeling overwhelmed, surrounded by books and notes and not sure where to begin. Around ten o'clock at night I called upon William Blake to help me and within minutes found myself writing feverishly until five in the morning, when it was finally complete. Throughout that night I kept calling upon him to point me in the right direction for a quote or passage of writing, and I would open a book at random and there it would be. I rushed into college that morning and handed it in to my literature tutor, telling him that I had been helped by William Blake. Fortunately, by this time they knew all about Spirit and me and didn't find it strange! I ended up with a 2:1, something I don't think I could have managed alone.

This was such an extraordinary time in my life when I was so happy and fulfilled, enjoying my degree course, the Rainbow groups and meeting new Spirit family just as the Spirit friends had said we would. My children were doing well and were happy back in the North of England. It was a period of tremendous flowering and discovery where I was introduced to more great masters of literature, philosophy and art. From Shakespeare and Leonardo da Vinci, to Mahler, Beethoven, and Mozart – all were part of the inspirational 'Work' brought to Earth. It was my friend John at college who introduced me to classical music. The first time I heard Mahler's 'Symphony of a Thousand' I cried.

Gradually, through my exposure to all these new ideas and influences, I was learning that experience of Spirit was not confined to a small working-class family in the North, but that we were part of a wider community that included not just teachers like Swedenborg and Rudolf Steiner, but artists and writers like Leonardo and William Blake.

There was a tremendous sense of expansion and abundance in my life at this time, a large part of which was the work that continued in the Rainbow Group. Paul was by now central to the group's activities and he and our other dear friend, Clive, worked closely together devising the spiritual development and consciousness-expansion work-shops. Several times a week we would meet and have an evening where we would go on a sort of mental pilgrimage. Whatever Mam initiated in these groups was ahead of its time and was to find its perfect expression in an extraordinary occur-rence right here on our doorstep in Rivington on 17 August 1987.

Mam was sixty-five when she walked 1,190 feet up in the dark to Rivington Pike, along with a gathering of her Rainbow Group members, to arrive at dawn to welcome in the Harmonic Convergence. The Harmonic Convergence was a worldwide spiritual event. People all over the world were meeting on hills, mountains and sacred sites.

Across the globe, people gathered in high places, believing that if 144,000 people came together in prayers for peace then it would make a significant change in global consciousness. All over the world, in places from Mount Shasta, California, to Stonehenge and the Glastonbury Tor in England, thousands met to welcome in a new era of peace. Many people who had studied Asian, European and Mayan astrology and prophecy had realised this date was very significant because of the unusual alignment of the planets. Others thought that peace would follow if 144,000 chosen people resonated together at this time. 'Thought is a living thing' was now being preached everywhere and people were acting upon it on both a personal and collective level.

Sir George Trevelyan, Fourth Baronet and great pioneer of New-Age thinking, joined in the Harmonic Convergence on that date too. Sir George had espoused crystal and angel therapy along with the power of ley lines and the importance of organic farming back in the 1940s, long before it was fashionable. He chose to climb up Glastonbury Tor, a place of legend, which rises up from the comparatively flat Somerset landscape and is said to be the meeting point of powerful ley lines. Its varied mythology includes claims that Joseph of Arimathea visited the area, bringing the Holy Grail, and that it is the true historical site of some of the King Arthur stories. We were to meet George Trevelyan a year later and hear his inspiring talk.

Trevelyan, incidentally, was a great friend and supporter of Eileen and Peter Caddy and Dorothy Maclean, who worked together to establish the Findhorn spiritual community in Scotland in 1972 – the place where our friend Clive had met the Rev Michael Stanley. Eileen Caddy was very like my mam in her simple faith and her personal relationship with God. Straightforward and unassuming, she helped countless people in her quiet way.

The night before the Harmonic Convergence we had stayed up all night doing meditations and prayers in preparation for our 3 a.m. start up to the Pike. When the sun came up we were all facing east and Mam said a simple prayer to God, giving thanks for being part of the loving thoughts that were now going around the world. She said she was witnessing what the Spirit friends had told her about all those years before and had never lost faith that it would happen. The work of Spirit was spreading and coming into the mainstream. She quietly played her part with her little band of seven people she loved at dawn on 17 August. These people – Paul and John (my fellow students from college), Clive, Martha, her two children and me – were with her that day and it was a memory I shall hold dear for ever. We 'felt' Spirit that morning and felt too our kindred spirits all over the planet.

By now, the Rainbow Group that my Mam started had about thirty members who would come and go, some continuing The Work in new forms. We were all being trained to be receptive and creative rather than being trained to be mediums in the Spiritualist sense. This was what the New Age movement was progressing towards. Central to this new form of communication was an equal participation on the spiritual level rather than being told what to believe by a priest or a medium. It was about being authentic and 'becoming spiritual,' working towards a direct personal experience of Spirit rather than the tired belief that simply by being a member of a particular religion mankind would be saved.

Spiritual movements are about finding the spirit within, and not just speaking of loving your enemy, but actually doing it. Spirituality is now about encouraging democracy and valuing everyone, especially those we don't want to accept as a society. Like the progressive Spiritualism of my Mam's time, the New Age movement valued everyone, whatever their creed, colour, ethnicity or sexual orientation. And with New Age spiritual retreats springing up everywhere at this time, it was certainly connecting with people on a bigger scale than ever before.

Interestingly, Mam and I met Eileen Caddy, one of the founders of the Findhorn spiritual community, when she was giving a talk in Lancaster

in the 1980s, and I was struck by their physical
and spiritual similarities. They both took great
care in their appearance, had a warm and inviting
presence and a simple philosophy of love and faith.
Like Mam, Eileen had experienced difficult times,
had made mistakes in her personal life and been
judged for them. But throughout their lives they
stayed true to God.

These women, born just a few years apart,
pioneered a new way of being. They both had a
deeply personal relationship with their God that
was not bound up in conventional religious affili-
ations, and they both looked within to find not
just a belief but the divine Spirit itself. They strived
to teach us to develop ourselves, to take the internal
journey to our higher selves which, once found,
would become a way of life. By bringing about the
creation of the Findhorn spiritual community,
Eileen Caddy helped thousands of people from all
over the world to look within for their God and
learn to love unconditionally. Like my mam, Eileen
Caddy is one of the people who helped me to love,
to forgive, to keep faith and to listen to the voice
within.

They are now both in Spirit and no doubt
continuing their loving ministry.

The year I turned forty, 1988, was such a big
year for me. It was the year I managed to get a 2.1
Honours Degree and the year I met Simon, my
husband-to-be. I know now that meeting Simon

was destined, even though neither of us would have chosen the other at the time. Until that point neither of us really knew what was right for us and I believe there was a good deal of Spirit intervention in our meeting.

As always, when it involves Spirit guidance, synchronicity plays a big part. Carl Jung, a psychoanalyst of the twentieth century, had coined the term 'synchronicity' to describe spiritual coincidence. In other words, when the soul has a need that will aid in its awakening, the solution will appear, whether that be in the form of a new teacher coming into your life, or a book, or a sign. In modern-day terms it is called the Law of Attraction. This magnetic energy was drawing many new inspiring people and things into my life at this time and it was a very exciting period.

My Literature tutor from college was getting married in the Lake District in the summer of 1988. Although we were friends, I think the invitation to his wedding may also have been to do with the fact that I could transport another guest to the event in my old banger. The reception was in the garden. It was a lovely sunny day and I spent most of it talking to the sister of the bride. We hit it off immediately, just like other kindred spirits I have been destined to meet. We had a lot in common, both being single mums with two grown-up children. Daphne told me of her dream to go to Crete and asked if I fancied going too. I certainly needed a holiday after many years of going without. I had just got my degree and had a few weeks remaining before I needed to look for a job and I was sure Mam would lend me the money.

Daphne said she would take care of all the arrangements and be in touch. True to her word, she rang and asked if she could bring along two friends, Simon and Andrew. I agreed, and with the money provided by Mam and Dad, we set the date to meet at Manchester Airport bound for a week in Crete. I was about to go on holiday with three strangers and I hoped I would remember what Daphne looked like.

My daughter Joanne was excited for me and ironed and helped me to pack. Then, as now, I was leaving things to the last minute and was in a bit of a flap. Jo and her boyfriend took me to the airport and I waved as I saw Daphne coming towards me. It wasn't the best start to my friendship with Simon as, with his view of me obscured, he assumed, and probably hoped, I was my eighteen-year-old daughter, shaking her hand with the words, 'Hello Pam!' However, after a week of the kind of in-depth honesty that happens in holiday conditions, helped along by liberal doses of Mataxa, we came together and I had met the love of my life.

For much of my life I have lived delightfully and

happily in the Now as we were all intended to do. Conversely, when I was not enjoying the moment, I was anxious, negative and worried about past and future events, going over old hurts in my head time and time again. All these mind games create negativity and dis-ease. Now, as I became close to Simon, I remembered the Spirit friends' early advice: *thought is a living thing*!

Simon and I married on the Summer Solstice, 21 June 1990. At that time Mam was sixty-eight, and a group of us walked up Rivington, leaving home at 3 a.m. again to be at the Pike for dawn to have a spiritual blessing of our marriage. We all stood in a circle and Mam led the service with a prayer and a blessing.

It was misty and we didn't see the sun rise, but it was very atmospheric and magical. We had asked everyone to bless our union with a flower. Each one came and gave us their flower and said a few words about what the flower represented. Everyone had given some thought to which flower they should choose and they each intuited what the flower meant for our union. It was very special and we were surrounded by many unseen friends from the Spirit world. Later that morning we had the official ceremony at the Spiritualist Church, which felt very personal too. It was a day to remember and those flowers and words meant so much more than any expensive wedding present we might have received.

With my degree under my belt, I wanted to start my teacher training, but first I needed to earn some money to supplement my grant, so I took a temporary job as a day centre officer with adults with learning difficulties. It turned out to be a fortunate move: I loved the job and was offered a permanent post, and soon after was seconded on day release to train as a social worker, abandoning my initial desire to become a teacher. I was on a salary while studying for my diploma in social work, which made things easier, as I was still supporting my two teenage children. When I qualified, I decided to specialise in the field of young children with disabilities, and their families. I never did get to teach but I continued my working life helping children.

Meanwhile my mother was at the height of her energies, and in 1990, after years of serving the Church in many capacities – committee work, as a greeter, organising jumble sales and running the Lyceum, amongst other thing – she was voted by the Church's members to become President of the Horwich Church. She was sixty-eight years of age and she was to serve for four years before her sudden death shortly before her seventy-second birthday.

I once complained to Mam that I didn't like Wednesdays as nothing ever happened. 'Oh no,' she would say, 'I love Wednesdays, it's my bingo day.' Fitting then that she should die very suddenly of a heart attack doing what she loved. Her friend Alice remarked that on the morning of her death she had come out of the flat absolutely glowing. She had always taken care of her appearance, wearing skirts and heels, proud of her shapely legs. It was very important to my mam that she always looked lovely, with styled hair and smart clothes.

Prone to indigestion, Mam used to have to avoid onions as they played havoc with her system, but apparently that day she decided to have what she fancied: a beef and onion pie. After bingo, where she'd had a win, Mam said to Alice that she was feeling a bit queer, probably because of the onions, and wanted to wait a bit for everybody to go until they left the hall themselves.

They had already locked the front door by the time they rose to leave. Alice was trying to push through the back door, which seemed a bit stiff, when Mam got up and said she would try it. She pushed the door and went down never to get up again.

I remember how beautiful it was that day. I had been to visit a family in my capacity as a social worker and had stopped the car afterwards just to look at the view. It was when I got back to the office that the news came. None of us had seen it coming, except perhaps for Mam herself. In the weeks prior to her death, during sittings, she kept saying she was blocked. She said she could no longer channel Spirit energy in her usual way, and even though we took no notice, perhaps she knew what was coming.

Her funeral at the Spiritualist Church was like a royal occasion, absolutely packed to the brim with people she loved and who loved her. I arranged Mam's favourite yellow roses for her, not knowing at the time that these flowers are the symbols of Mother Mary. I have moving letters from people who came from all walks of life and had been touched by her light. On the evening of the funeral we talked of her immeasurable gifts; her ability to overcome adversity and to forgive herself and others. We remembered the wonderful circles, the Spirit messages always based on love, and her unconquerable faith in Spirit and The Work. We told family stories and laughed, we sang her favourite songs and heard her favourite poems – it was as if we could feel Spirit celebrating the life of this extraordinary woman who had no qualifications or money and whose only worldly goods were her treasured letters and photographs.

We had always been waiting for The Work to start and could not conceive that Mam wouldn't be around when it happened. We waited and waited and though we never lost faith, it was a shock when Mam died and The Work hadn't materialised. Surely she had to be there when the great moment arrived?

Although we had been told that the two worlds would come together in the twinkling of an eye, we hadn't really given much thought to what would precede this new change. Neither had we given any thought to the preparation or state of global consciousness necessary to achieve this momentous event.

Seventeen days after Mam died, I sat on the bed looking out into the garden, feeling the most unbearable loss. I cried my heart out for Mam and asked God for the insufferable pain to end. I really couldn't bear it.

Then out of the blue an energy came that filled me and stilled me. This unearthly feeling of love and peace descended just as it had all those years earlier when I had travelled down the tunnel of light. Again I was given a beautiful gift from Spirit to help me – I was given a vision of Mam's continuation of Spirit and her mission.

In this state, I knew her time had come to move onto greater things and I understood that my personal loss and pain was nothing compared to The Work that was continuing for our soul group. I realised that all humanity was here to bring about the awakening as to who and what we truly are. I also knew that when we return to Spirit after death we start to prepare again for our next incarnation, or to work from Spirit guiding those who return to the Great Forgetting of this material realm. On that day, Saturday 29 October, 1994, I felt compelled to write this revelation down, and then locked it away in a drawer in my room where it stayed until eleven years later when I began writing this book; only then did I fully understand what it meant. This is a copy of what I wrote that day:

I could not feel her close to me and I sensed she was working spiritually far away. A peace descended and I was aware that she had gone to Spirit to complete her work. She was working and linking up with great spiritual masters in Peru. She had been a shepherdess here, nurturing us and keeping us linked with our tribe. Having done that, she now had to transcend the physical and do much greater work in her much higher state.

Because her passing had been recent she was able to communicate on both the lower vibrations of the earth plane and the higher vibrations of the spiritual dimensions. Her job is now to link the Spirit people of Peru to the people who have reincarnated into bodies. The Spirit people of Peru are neither dead nor alive in the sense that we understand these states in our present form. They are so highly evolved or transcended that they do not experience a separation between their physical and spiritual mind.

They have not died to become pure Spirits as we must do. They have evolved into this state. Thus they cannot enter our lower dimension because they exist on a much higher vibration than we do. They are therefore linking up to 'beacons' in the physical matter through rebirth, in order to continue the Great Work. However, it is a risky business and even though we are guided and helped to awaken, we can so easily become lost in matter. Beacons will be transmitters, channels to and from (our?) people in Peru. My mother is linking our group so that direct communication can be transmitted to the people of this world of dense matter. We shall remember who we are and why we are here.

I prayed, offering my self, my life, to this service.

The work of millions of years is now upon us.

All we have to do is to be open, to record and share with those who are in our tribal group.

To meditate, pray and offer our lives to spiritualising this planet.

It does not matter where we are physically; it is where we are inside ourselves.

My mother's death heralds this fruition. Let us be ready to integrate our Spirit mind and body to the world.

I was awakening and after all these years I was finally beginning to understand that for the great changes to happen it is not just up to the Spirit world, but instead, humanity itself has to be equally ready to take the return journey back to the light, using not only the heart and intuition but also the rational mind. New thought and the drive of the Spirit were leading us back to the inner realms of our being. Timing is crucial to The Work and it *will* happen in the twinkling of an eye when the worlds are on the same vibration. I believe we are not far away from this alignment and as more of us awaken to our Spirit collectively, we receive and transmit thoughts of love and light.

My mother often comes through to me quite clearly these days and I feel her at my shoulder as I write this: WE ARE EMERGING!

After Mam's death, I stayed a little while longer at the Spiritualist Church, but I realised that my attendance there had been as much about helping her run the church as anything else. I attended the Spiritualist Church as a healer for fourteen years, and I always considered it to be an honour to be part of the group and to feel the presence of healing angels. But at the end of that time I felt I had to move on. I continued to practise as an absent healer through prayer and will still help now if I am specifically asked for healing.

However, there were other things pressing in and demanding my time. I had a full-time job working with children with profound disabilities and their families, which I loved. Every day I saw unbelievable courage, tenacious commitment, tears of anxiety and exhaustion, as well as tears of joy and laughter when a child achieved one of the little milestones that most of us take for granted. I saw the incredible spirit of these children and their families, but most of all I came to learn that the greatest thing any of us have is love.

I also had the trip of a lifetime to organise: a pilgrimage to America to visit some of the places important to the indigenous people. All my life, three philosophies have hugely influenced me – socialism, Spiritualism and the sacred way of life of the indigenous tribes of America. I am not sure how it originally came about, but since childhood I have had a fascination for Native American culture and religion. As I mentioned previously, many early Spiritualist mediums worked with Native American Spirit guides. Indeed, I am told that when my mam developed her trance mediumship, it was an America Indian who was the first to 'come through'.

I believe that the ancient souls of the indigenous peoples have been teaching us their wisdom since passing to the higher life, where they continue their sacred communion with us. I believe that they are now our Spirit guides who influence and inspire us. I am also certain that Indian Spirits have returned to this realm through reincarnation to show us how to live in harmony and balance with Mother Earth and the Great Spirit, Wakan Tanka.

The culmination of all my years of fascination with Native American Spiritualism came in 1996 when I fulfilled a life-long dream to go on a pilgrimage to South Dakota. Simon and I spent the first few days at the Star Nation Conference where American Indians and indigenous folk from all over the world came to share their wisdom. We heard some wonderful talks about living in harmony with the Great Spirit and how the people were renewing their old healing ways. We heard myths and stories passed down from their ancestors and it was an altogether inspiring and wonderful experience.

In the audience was the late Dr John Mack, an American professor of psychiatry at Harvard Medical School, who was interested in humanity's ability to transform consciousness. I had read his books and I was delighted to meet him here too.

While we were in America we spent two weeks walking in the Black Hills of Dakota in the footsteps of the great chiefs and holy men of the Plains Indians. The Black Hills provide a breathtaking backdrop to this historically significant site and I was so captivated by Sylvan Lake that many years later when I was asked to imagine the best possible funeral I might have during a meditation, Lake Sylvan came to mind. I 'saw' all my loved ones both in Spirit and in body holding hands around the lake, singing and celebrating my passing, and of course my Spirit was there too, joyfully joining in.

Not far from Mount Rushmore was a wonderful

tribute to Crazy Horse, the legendary Oglala Lakota warrior and great leader. He has been immortalised in an enormous monumental carving hewn from the face of a mountain in the Black Hills. The monument was started in 1948 by the Polish sculptor Korczak Ziolkowski, at the request of Henry Standing Bear and other elders. After Ziolkowski's death, his widow continued the still-unfinished work. When completed it will show Crazy Horse astride his horse, pointing out across the plains. The site is now a centre of Native American culture and learning. To give you some idea of the scale, the carving is so huge that the Mount Rushmore carvings of American presidents would easily fit on Crazy Horse's forehead.

We continued onto to Bear Butte, a mountain of great sacredness to the local Plains Indians. It is a place where many tribes, past and present, come to vision-quest, offer prayers, meditate and conduct ceremonies. We walked this beautiful mountain in a silence befitting its sacred nature and status. The Lakota people call it Mato Paha, or Bear Mountain.

Our final destination was Mateo Tipi or Bear Lodge, another sacred site some seventy miles to the north-west in Wyoming. This is the national monument that was featured in the film *Close Encounters of the Third Kind*, but for the indigenous people it is a place of great spiritual presence.

When we arrived we were stunned into silence. It completely stilled us, as though we were enveloped in an invisible power and suspended in time. We just sat there for an hour, spellbound, looking at this solidified core of an ancient volcano that had risen out of the ground and stands like a monument to God.

There is a legend that tells of seven young girls being chased by a bear. When they prayed to be saved by the Great Spirit, the ground beneath them started to rise and they found themselves five hundred feet in the air looking down on the beautiful surrounding land. The bear, heartbroken and frustrated, started to claw the sides of the mountain, giving it the characteristic markings we see today. The girls, grateful for their salvation, were then lifted up to the heavens and became the 'Seven Sisters' or Pleiades constellation in the northern night sky. This place was so magnetic that we made the return five-hour journey just to see it at night, with billions of stars twinkling overhead.

I returned from South Dakota feeling replenished and in tune with a part of me that had always been longing to connect to the sacred land of the Lakota Sioux.

Before I went I had been saddened to think we had lost something for ever. I believed that the culture of this great nation – their religion, language, ceremony, dance and way of life – had been annihilated in a very short time when the young American pioneers let their newfound freedom and material greed get the better of them.

But I came back feeling quite differently. Not only was there a renewal by the young Native Americans in all matters relating to their spiritual connectedness and the wisdom of their spiritual ancestors, I also felt the presence of their ancestors still very much alive in the land. In the sacred places where the ancient ones had communed with Wakan Tanka, the Great Spirit, I felt their Spirits waiting for us to join them. When I was in the Black Hills, at Sylvan Lake and at Mateo Tipi, I 'felt' a presence so powerful that it immediately connected me to the Spirit within and without, beyond the need for prayer or thoughts. The best way I can describe this is to say it was a communion with the light.

On our trip I heard about prophecies the sacred holy men of the tribes had made, long before the white man came. A holy man of the Oglala Sioux, Black Elk – the man who was born in 1863, the same year as my Great Grandfather and who visited Salford in 1887 – foresaw a time when their way of life would disappear, but he also saw a time when all nations would unite again. There is a legend that when the sacred White Buffalo returns, it will herald a time of world peace and unity. After my connection with this Holy Land I had no doubt that it won't be long!

Within a few weeks of our return from Dakota I

was blessed with another very powerful connection. I was in work when the call came. It was in the October, two years after Mam had passed, when the first of my three beautiful granddaughters arrived. The moment I saw her I felt an incredible love for this tiny, helpless baby, who I had never seen before but who was already linked to my heart from times past. I was to have the same wonderful soul recognition on the first meeting with all three of my granddaughters.

I believe the young of today are bringing a new light and breaking old barriers and patterns that will take us more swiftly into the new heaven on earth. They will no doubt challenge the status quo, making parental roles more difficult. Caring for these sensitive, receptive and dynamic old souls will force us to reflect on how we minister our care. They are here to teach and to reveal so much.

For eleven years my life was very busy. I had a job that took up all my time, working with families and children who have special needs. My evenings and weekends were gladly taken up with the babies and the remaining elders of my family. There was little time to go to church but I continued with my daily prayers and chats to Mam and Spirit. The Rainbow groups continued every Friday night, although many members were now scattered all over the country.

As the needs of my elders entailed a lot of

travelling, and I was also facing an increasing workload, I was becoming increasingly stressed, bursting into tears at the slightest problem. It never occurred to me to slow down. One night, my friend Joyce invited me to meet a friend of hers who was visiting from Canada. We all met up in a restaurant and as usual I was smiling, being sociable and covering up the awful foreboding I felt. For some time I had been trying to ignore a tight ball of stress in my chest. I felt that if I acknowledged it, it would take over, and I didn't want to lose control. I had to keep going. Making small talk, the visitor asked me what I did for a living. In the space of a moment, in the middle of a busy restaurant, I started to cry uncontrollably. My friends had the wisdom to let me get it all out without trying to comfort or stop me.

I remember the lady's words clearly when she said, 'Why don't you just stop?'

It was a revelation. People like me didn't do that. We didn't chuck in perfectly good jobs just because we were finding it hard to cope. But this lady had lost everything she valued. Her husband of thirty years had left, she'd become ill, lost her job and eventually her beautiful home and all the possessions they had worked so hard all their lives to accumulate. From the greatest pain imaginable she had somehow managed to find herself and the love within, which no money could ever buy. We went our separate ways at the end of the evening but this earth angel changed my life. I took some time off from work, and although I tried again a couple of times, eventually I came to accept that I had to stop altogether.

I walked for hours on my beloved Rivington. I tried to concentrate on breathing deeply and properly, something I realised I hadn't done for a long time. It was as if I had been holding my breath for years. Walking in the Japanese gardens, up Rivington Pike and by the reservoirs brought me back to myself. I was healing, and Simon, my family and granddaughters did the rest through their love and joy.

The next few years were a wonderful gift where I had the opportunity just to relax and enjoy my life. I was able to spend more time with my two dads, my father-in-law and the other elderly relatives. I was to have the privilege of being with some of them when they left their outworn bodies, and met with their waiting loved ones. I also had one beautiful gift from Spirit within a few years of Mam's passing that helped me to prepare four more of our elders to pass in the following years.

My dad's brother, Uncle Fred, was a lifelong Spiritualist and epitomised the teachings of Spiritualism. Fred and his wife Bella only joined the circles in the early 1980s. They had been prevented from joining the first sittings because of Fred's stint in the Army. A tireless fundraiser for the Church, he attended services regularly and was a good friend to many. He walked with Spirit every moment of his existence, greeting everyone he met with cheer and respect. The phrase 'Hail fellow, well met' comes to mind, and just being around him used to make me happy. He and Auntie Bella would visit lonely elderly people for a chat and to see if they needed anything. He lived his life in service and made many people merry with his famous home-brew.

Fred also cared deeply for the children of the world and couldn't bear to think of them going hungry. For his birthday, he asked relatives to give him money rather than presents so that he could give it to the charity, Save the Children. Fred was a socialist, even more passionate than my Dad. A man before his time in many ways, he had been a vegetarian all his adult life, unheard of in those days in the North.

He was also forever reading about healing and cures as a way round taking his medication. For instance, one day he read that in ancient times nettles had been used on the skin to cure many ailments. I can't remember what he was suffering from at the time but without delay he fetched some nettles and asked Bella to do the honours. What followed was the worst night of his life. In the morning, thinking a bath might soothe him, he stepped into the water only to find it made it ten times more painful. He concluded that nettles must have been different in ancient times.

Although a jokey character by nature, Fred had total belief in Spirit and life after death. I was fortunate to be with him when he died and although he was not conscious in the accepted sense, I knew he was talking to me and I could tell he was finding it hard to leave because he was worried about his wife, Auntie Bella. He had loved and looked after her so much.

Eventually he had to break free and be received into the world of Spirit. I closed my eyes and saw him walking through a hole in the wall and along a corridor where my mam was calling to him. She kept repeating, 'Come, Fred, she will be all right, she will be looked after.' He went slowly and reluctantly at first, but as he got nearer to Mam he looked like the Uncle Fred we had always known. He was walking again with renewed and joyful energy and had left his unbearable pain behind. He was still attached to his body by a cord and it stretched as he walked away. Then an incredible sight came to me – Fred's father, my paternal granddad, who had died before I was born, arrived on a motorbike and my mam disappeared. Although I had never met my grandfather, I knew it was him. He was smiling at Fred. I heard him say, 'Come on, Fred, I'm taking you to see all those children you have worried about all your life.' Uncle Fred got on the back of his bike and I watched as they rode up a beautiful hill through lush green countryside. They were so happy on their way to the children's realm and the further they receded into the distance, the thinner the cord became, until it gently faded into nothing and he was as free as the wind.

Uncle Fred had met Simon a few years earlier and they had became great pals. Fred had said that because Simon was 'th'only one that talks proper in our family', he wanted him to conduct his funeral. This Simon did and has continued to do so for many of our family and friends at the Spiritualist Church. Because he knows them so well and he works so lovingly on his presentation, his funerals have been the most wonderful, personal celebrations of these characters' lives.

Then, out of the blue in 2005, came a dramatic unfolding to my life. I had an awakening over a nine-month period. The awakening took the form of dreams and visions and the inspirational writing that would result in *Hope Street*. For five years I was led by a series of synchronicities to people, places, books and life experiences, which furthered my understanding and my capacity to love and see the world in a completely different way. Being led this way was as though a light had been switched on and I have walked continually in delight with this loving power, knowing that it would never let me down.

Part Four

The Work

In retrospect it is clear that my whole life has been a preparation for the time when I would write *Hope Street* and share our experiences of Spirit, but only now can I see that. In 2005 I was very happy with life as it was. I was retired, had three gorgeous granddaughters on whom I doted, and a lovely husband and extended family. I looked forward to a wonderful future with my family and friends, just pottering around the house and garden or roaming up Rivington, free from the stress of working life. I had yet to 'receive' the many wonderful insights from Spirit that were to come during that significant nine-month gestation period. During that time I was to write thousands upon thousands of words that would change my world. I still have wonderful times with my lovely family but I am afraid that pottering is on the back burner. It has proved to be a radical and enlightening change of direction, which has brought much inspiration and fulfilment at a time in my life when most people are gently slowing down.

I missed my mam dreadfully after she died in 1994, not only because was she my mam, but because she was my mentor, my friend and a bridge to our wonderful Spirit friends. Life was not empty, though. At that time I had a job in social work that I loved and a very busy life spending time with the remaining elders of the family and my beautiful granddaughters. Then in the spring of 2005, totally out of the blue, I began to have these dreams and visions, and I felt a renewed and more profound relationship with Spirit. Although I had never abandoned my spiritual life, what was happening now was unprecedented, forceful and dramatic.

I started waking at 5 a.m. full of energy, and had to rush downstairs to start writing. I even had to learn how to use a computer in order to keep up with my thoughts. Until then I had stubbornly resisted modern technology but my handwriting could not keep up with the thoughts flooding my mind. I was experiencing an uncommon energy and even had to sleep with a pad and pen by the bed, as it was not unusual for me to wake bolt upright at 2 a.m. and have to write down visions that had come to me in my dreams.

These were radical, enlightening thoughts that sometimes seemed to bear more relation to science fiction than spiritual inspiration. Thousands and thousands of words came pouring out over the following months and at the time I was convinced that those words were not mine but channelled through me by Spirit. I now know that it was more of a communion with Spirit and that all the material was inside of me, ready to awaken when the time was right. I also know that this inner life and knowledge is not only within me but it is universal and is within everyone.

As I write it is August 2010, and I finally have clarity about all the dreams and visions I received during that extraordinary nine-month period in 2005.

I have total trust in everything I learned because I received it with love and compassion. It was the same unconditional love I had felt for Jesus at the end of the tunnel. It was what I had searched for in all manner of ways throughout my life.

Whilst I was receiving I was in a state of what I can only describe as high energy. I was living in a state of divine imagination and other worldliness. I felt like Alice in Wonderland.

I would like to share with you a small part of my spiritual adventure that continues to this day, from which I know there is no going back. In fact now this shining path has been opened, life will never be the same, and this path is there waiting to welcome everyone. Not only is it waiting, it becomes exponential, more magnetic and attractive in its radiance, as each one of us steps consciously on the return path back to the oneness of love and abundance we all attempt to find materially.

Every morning when I was receiving I would awake before dawn, go downstairs and be compelled to write. At this stage I couldn't use a computer and I would try, with difficulty, to keep up with the inspiration coming, writing longhand and later in the day dictating to my husband, Simon, as he typed. I had retired just before computers were being used in the workplace but in a very short time I was proficient in using the keyboard, such was the motivation to receive and record quickly.

Every morning I would write for about three hours, and then continue my normal routine in a very ordinary way. I was a very ordinary woman having an extraordinary spiritual experience.

I ask you to keep an open mind, but not without discernment. Everyone has their own unique path, planned before they returned to this material world. Along this path you will awaken to the divine light within. This awakening may happen through dreams and visions or through the love you give and receive from the beautiful children who are here on earth to lead us. You may awaken through pain and adversity as you let go of patterns that no longer serve you. Whatever route we are taking, our divine self is waking us up from a long sleep of total identification with our limited, material self.

The visions that came to me were to rouse me from my deep slumber. My interpretations of the visions and the writings that follow should not be viewed as true or untrue because anything that can be 'thought' is transient. My family history and my life experiences have shaped me and will have influenced my interpretations, in the same way that any individual might interpret them differently according to their own life story. But the feeling of love and oneness that accompanied these experiences is a constant and cannot be dismissed. I was sure that The Work had started its final manifestations towards the huge leap in consciousness humanity was about to take.

I received messages for nine months, but I know that what I received is within each one of us. The script may be different but the destination remains the same. I started to experience these dreams and visions following my decision to write about my mam's mediumship. Some of them were more like science fiction fantasies and involved the purple people from the fifth dimension, but they had that same loving, driving energy about them that had accompanied any communion with Spirit and angels in the past. It was almost as if opening up to tell my mother's story had activated and released all this new material. When I feel Spirit around me I get really excited, and nothing appears impossible.

'Shall I write two books, one factual about Mam's mediumship and the other a science fiction novel?' I asked my husband.

My enthusiasm and naivety amused Simon. I was not an author let alone able to write two books! He loves my joy and enthusiasm, however, and in his patient but never patronising way said, 'Why not just sit down and write all that's in your head and see what happens?' As always, he was right.

I looked at the blank page, said a prayer to the Divine Light and then put pen to paper:

'Dedicated to my mother

10 October 2005, 11 a.m.'

Then suddenly, and out of the blue, flowing from my pen came:

'ALPHA & OMEGA: THE AWAKENING'

Where did that come from? I had not even considered a title, let alone one so grand, but it had written itself. The title implied much more than I had intended or even knew.

Going back in time I remembered the Spirit friends saying, 'When The Work starts, you will know because you "shall come into your own" and have an inner knowing. Listen to your intuition, follow your inner voice, and watch for signs of confirmation from Spirit.'

Reflecting on this, I pondered. Was The Work a global event as indicated by the Spirit messages given all those years ago, or was it an individual awakening? Maybe both! Yes, of course, it could not be any other way.

I then remembered a meditation I'd had years before when, from out of the silence, I had received a simple but profound thought that had stayed with me:

'HEAL YOURSELF AND YOU HEAL THE WORLD.'

Of course, it was that simple! All each one of us needed to do was to heal ourselves and together we could heal the world. But of course it would need everyone to take responsibility for putting things right for themselves and not passing the buck. And what did 'heal yourself' mean anyway?

I have always thought that problems arise from the deep loss we all feel inside ourselves, which has resulted from our physical perception that we are separate from the Source. As a result of this separation at our soul's core, we always feel hurt, rejected and unloved.

Always craving oneness, which is our birthright, we continually search outside ourselves for love, approval and fulfillment, and when that fails, which is inevitable, we blame, judge, feel hurt, rejected and unloved all over again. This compounds the ego's belief that we are alone and unconnected and that life has to be suffered.

Feeling powerless, misunderstood and alone in our ego state, but still having the inherent drive for oneness, we continue the unhealthy cycle of being hurt, hurting, blaming and creating chaos. What is more, we then take these hurts into our mind and put them on 'playback' until we are full of anger, hatred and resentment all over again. Just the right environment for the ego to justify taking revenge on its enemy!

Writing all these thoughts down as quickly as I could, I read back what I had scrawled and could not believe that I had come up with this wisdom. It had just flowed. Everyone should try this. It's amazing what is inside of us and what is given from Spirit. Just try asking yourself a question you would ask a Spiritual Master and you will be surprised at what you hold within.

I was attending workshops and seminars on spiritual matters that just a few years before would have comprised a handful of people. Now, they were packing huge conference halls. This state of being resonated very strongly with what the Spirit friends had told us about people coming into their own, desiring a different world and wanting to change their perception. All signs that Spirit had told us to expect when The Work was nearing its completion.

'You will meet and recognise the Spirits of your soul group who have also returned to do The Work,' we had been told all those years ago. Certainly there is no doubt in my mind that the reincarnation of more and more powerful light entities to this dimension are proof that The Work is nearing the end of this cycle, when the two worlds would unite as we had been told in 1953.

Although my mother's death was the most painful experience, I never lost touch or faith in Spirit, and every day I meditated, sent healing prayers, particularly for the children of the world, and offered myself in service to The Work. Faith in The Work is at the core of my very being. I also continued to communicate daily with Mam in thought and prayer. Now, eleven years after my mother's passing, I was being filled with new and unusual insights and was compelled to share them. I was being led on this wonderful journey of awakening, being given little pearls of wisdom, inspiration and gifts from all directions. I was also meeting people who would inspire me to new levels of awareness and because of this I, too, became inspiring. I now knew that nothing was ever accidental in my life. When one becomes aware of being more than the 'little material me' and gets in touch with the soul identity, synchronicity starts to operate. It was as if I had stepped into another world where the path was shining brightly for me to follow.

I lived in total trust and as I became aware of my existence in this 'other world', more and more was revealed to me. Every moment, signs of confirmation would appear from people, Spirit, angels, books, music and dreams. I was like a magnet, attracting all that I needed to further my awakening.

It was so amazing and extraordinary, yet I knew I could depend on it, and every day I waited in anticipation for the next shining and delightful signpost. I felt totally awake, joyful and transformed. It seemed that my joy and expectancy ensured the results in abundance. This is how life should be, so awake. It is there for us all to tap into if we think on the right wavelength! Suddenly as I wrote the word 'wavelength', the beautiful energy I am coming to recognise returns again and I am offered further enlightenment on this inspiration.

'You speak of Synchronicity leading you. Have you considered that it might be *YOU* that is leading?

You are literally a conductor of your own symphony.

You are now aware that you are a receptor, a beacon emitting light.

Just by being in this radiant consciousness enables you to be in the field of energy that pervades everything.

Whether you call it Spirit or energy or light or the life force, it is you and you are not separate from it. You are the thing in itself.

By your observation, your recognition *of* "*It*", you become "*It*".

YOU ARE IT!'

In that moment I truly perceived from my heart why Spirit had given me the title '*Alpha and Omega: The Awakening*'.

I had previously understood 'thought is a living thing' to mean that we should be careful not to have harmful thoughts because we hurt others, and that as a result the negativity comes back to us. But now I really understand that it is so much more. 'Thought is a living thing' literally means that we are so powerful, we create reality. We *are* the synchronicity. Every thought has consequences, whether they are positive or negative, and the more passion behind the thought the greater the manifestation. Either we 'see' and 'act' from the limited perception or we 'see' and 'be' the Soul Identity.

Thus, we create fear or love, anxiety or peace, depression or happiness within ourselves and the world. We make that choice every moment, and the consequences are apparent.

I realised The Work was not about getting people to believe in reincarnation or life after death. The cycle of life and death and reincarnation is the 'Way of the Spirit' until we became light conscious.

It was not about believing or grasping it intellectually any more, rather it was '*being* it'. Thus, we could consciously understand and know how to use our immense divine power. In this state no one would need convincing of anything, we would be living it. Truly living the divine identity:

I AM

I would like to reiterate some things.

Fifty-seven years ago at the well-established home circle in Hope Street, The Work entered the consciousness of the sitters through the trance mediumship of my mam. I was a child when I learned about The Work. For as long as I can remember this knowledge has been present in me. Throughout the intervening years, until my Mam's passing forty years later, we were told the same straightforward things without any alterations or additions. There were a few simple principles to The Work:

The Work involved reincarnation but not of every soul that had ever lived.

In our lifetime great changes would occur for humanity, accompanied by man-made and natural disasters.

We would know when The Work was finally coming to fruition because we would 'come into our own'; we would 'know' things and know what to do.

The world would change in 'the Twinkling of an Eye' when the two worlds would come together.

Two things were paramount: *'Thought is a living thing'* and *'Keep faith in The Work'*.

These two statements were imprinted on my mind. They were the foundation of my life and they have ensured the publishing of this book. I know that finally, at the age of sixty-three, I shall be accomplishing what I was born to do. But I couldn't have done it alone. Not only have I been guided by my Spirit friends and angels, but I have been led by many kindred spirits here on the earth plane.

Spirit told me that I would meet people in my life and there would be an instant recognition with them. These people were our Spirit family here to further The Work. I would 'know' these people immediately and indeed I have, not in any physical, intellectual or rational way, but in an emotional sense. I recognised them by what I can only describe as recognising with their 'essence', which made me feel an amazing bond, a joy, oneness and incredible love. I am sure you have experienced this too.

All my life, The Work was in my heart and on my mind, sometimes right at the forefront of my mind and sometimes in the recesses, but never in all those years did I ever doubt or lose faith in it. For the past five years I have received further clarity and have thought of little else.

We were told that The Work had been going on for aeons but that this lifetime would see the final manifestations when we would 'come into our own' and the worlds would come together. I now think of 'coming into our own' as awakening to our true selves of light, and in so doing we perceive a new world, but one that has always been there. A great many people are awakening to what the mystics and holy people have always perceived.

First it is necessary for the individual to develop freedom of thought. I am certain that we are on the cusp of a huge leap in consciousness that was initiated in the age of enlightenment by a group of highly evolved light pioneers. Everything since has been leading to a time when humanity can be freed from oppression and in so doing empower the global change. Great thinkers led us to under- stand democratic and scientific concepts and to fight for equality and education. Not many years ago the majority of us could neither read nor write and had little time to think of anything else apart from survival. We have already come a long way.

They say history is one bloody thing after another and I am certain my grandma would have agreed with that, but consciousness does indeed evolve. Everything we have ever discovered and invented or desired is driven by the consciousness that is in service to enlightening our selves. These ideas and concepts are first of all conceived in the Spirit world before we are born into this plane of the great forgetting. It is our job to reconnect, remember and recognise our particular light group here with the help of Spirits and angels of light that guide us to meet with other kindred souls and then to awaken. When we do, the world as we know it shall change in the twinkling of an eye. It is not the case that we will go anywhere physically but instead we shall perceive a different world, a world that has always been there, vibrating on a higher vibration of light, waiting for us on another dimension where our higher self resides. As we become our higher self, we are light conscious and the new world will become visible. In the act of seeking, we shall find.

I was made aware of many insights. We reveal ourselves in every conceivable thing. We invent materially what we already *are* in Spirit. For instance, we started with smoke signals, letters and the telegraph in our drive for communication and now we have mobile phones and e-mail, giving instant communication worldwide, as near to telepathy as we can get. The radio and television, like ourselves, send and receive invisible transmissions from their silicon crystals. The World Wide Web reveals our innate drive for connectedness. As our spirits come into their own at this time of revelation we see every kind of Re-United occurring on the internet, from Friends to Genes. Facebook is all part of The Work of connecting that these lovely young Spirits have come to do. Football is a very magnetic and passionate energy. Wherever you go in the world they have heard of Man United, and Unite Man they surely do. And of course, you too, City!

Dance and music and no end of universal and creative drives lead us to uncover our powerful creativity, joy and connectedness beyond race, creed and language. The language we all have in common is the language of love.

Franz Mesmer – the eighteenth-century physicist who believed in a natural energetic transference between all things – was a pioneer who led Freud and Jung on the path of the self-consciousness. As a result of their work, among others, the human race was being led to our inner space where we could reflect on our selves. We were guided to perceive ourselves as multidimensional. We devised sociology, psychology and anthropology in which to locate ourselves. We can now locate ourselves on our family tree and understand ourselves in terms of lineage and its effects. The tree, in all religions and esoteric knowledge, is a symbol of the human genome. We also have a massive interest in our ancestry, in seeking our roots. We are finding huge synchronicities in the paths of our ancestors and our selves. The 'Tree of Life' is appearing in the material realm so that we 'know' ourselves in our many roles and identities. The philosophers, the scientists and the reformers of the enlightenment have paved the way for this time when we, the masses, can all realise ourselves as individuals, as particles of the whole, and thereby make a collective decision to change the world. Ordinary people like us can do what only a handful of people did up to a few years ago, such as write, philosophise and have direct communion with the divine.

The unravelling of the mysteries of DNA has revealed the connectedness and oneness of everyone and everything physically. The beautiful double helix may yet reveal our spiritual counterpart. Geometry gives us a lot of clues to our sacred origins.

Now we have quantum physics, telescopes and microscopes, we are helped 'To see a world in a grain of sand, And a heaven in a wild flower, Hold infinity in the palm of your hand, And eternity in an hour. We now see what the mystics always knew intuitively. Science and mystical experience are coming closer.

Through technology we have the means to share and know the history of everything. We are being educated and enlightened rationally. We are learning about ourselves through love and fear, through joy and adversity, through reactions and choices. And in so doing we come to know ourselves as pilgrims on an awakening path. We can only truly perceive ourselves as a part of the whole when we have found our true self. Then the individual and the collective path become one and the same. Once we become conscious we may integrate the two.

The media shows us more than anywhere the big questions we are asking ourselves. Books and films reflect a state of consciousness that seeks to solve mysteries, secrets and conspiracy. The Dan Brown and Harry Potter books are only popular because we are hungry for the magic and mystery that we are ourselves. Many films are examining different states of reality, such as *Inception* and *The Matrix*. Others investigate the choices we make, the society in which we live and how this affects the hero within. Love and the lack of it is our greatest awakener.

Becoming a grandmother was the most powerful path to my awakening. The children of light entering the arena now have a very transforming energy and shall show us the way to a new heaven on earth. The love I experienced for and from these little ancient souls prepared the way for me for to perceive a path to a new world.

When I started receiving these visions, in 2005, I was compelled to start upon a path that would lead me eventually to having this book published, but at the time I had no idea where it would lead. I didn't make a conscious choice about anything, but the compulsion to follow these very powerful intuitions was irresistible.

I 'received' from what at the time I thought was outside of myself, from wonderful discarnate souls who were given the names of Enoch and Joshua. These two beings of light inspired me to 'ask and receive' and took me to wonderful places of vision. I was taken to the 'Crystal Dome' with Joshua and saw how we were all attached to the unseen world and to each other through light, which manifests here on this material plane in the colours of the rainbow spectrum. The night I first met Joshua was to change me forever.

As I lay in bed, drifting towards sleep, I felt an extraordinary feeling of love and elation. I then felt something incredible, as if a magnet had been placed at the top of my head and was pulling me gently. It was a gorgeous feeling that was irresistible and I abandoned myself to this new and yet strangely familiar feeling. My spine arched and suddenly I was free and light.

I looked down at two bodies sleeping on the bed and realised it was Simon and me. How strange to see myself as another person, as others see me. Just as I was studying myself, I noticed a shining cord attached from me to my sleeping body. The light in the cord was fluid and pulsating. Peering into the cord I saw a little scenario being played out. It was like watching a play but I realised I was watching myself, watching myself!

I was seeing myself peering into the cord watching my sleeping body that was also dreaming this exact scene also. How utterly strange and mesmerising it was. Was every experience, dream and thought recorded, stored and played back in this shining fluid lifeline? Was I seeing memory in action? This image and my questions were quickly lost at that moment as a far more powerful light and feeling came upon me and replaced the previous scene with an image of the cord magnified and expanded a hundredfold. I looked deeper into this expansive, fluid, living scene being created before my very eyes, and as I stared in unbelievable wonder, I was engulfed in a light of tender and enveloping love.

This heightened state reminded me of the light at the end of the tunnel all those years ago, only this time I hadn't gone through the dark place first. No longer an observer, I was now in the scene, being transported by this fluid, and there in front of me was a sight that took my breath away, filling me with delight and amazement.

There, glistening, sparkling and pulsating with life, was a beautiful Crystal Dome, resonating in sound and light, and shining with gold, silver and all the colours of the rainbow light. Not in my wildest dreams could I have imagined it, such was its exquisite and other-worldly beauty. Yet intuitively I knew that I was a particle of this exquisite, beautiful, living monument to the human spirit in its god-like proportions.

Being 'in the scene' didn't really describe what I felt. Again I experienced being 'the thing in itself'. I *was* the love; I was the light, the crystal, the sound, the colour and the beauty. I was at one with everything and everyone in that moment.

As I looked in absolute joy and delight, an ecstatic sense of awareness swept through me as the exquisite, magnetic love started to draw me in. I was engulfed, and becoming part of the structure of the dome. I was suddenly inside this expanding and infinite space, facing Joshua. How did I know his name or, for that matter, what he was thinking? This beautiful shining being – who seemed to emanate the highest essence of all human potential, whilst also lovingly encompassing diverse expressions of life such as gender, creeds and cultures – had entered my life. It was not for the first time. Joshua, I knew, was the Keeper of the Dome.

Joshua and I moved as one entity and experienced the many wondrous things the Dome had to impart. We didn't talk in the normal way, rather I communed with Joshua and the crystal, receiving wonderful insights and understanding appropriate to my present level of perception. This infinite Crystal Dome was vibrating and pulsating. It was the heart, the generator, the powerhouse of human consciousness. It transmitted light and sound to every living soul on earth, transported through the cord. This cord of living fluid was the super-conducting receptor that transported the light and sound. This receptive cord of creative fluid recorded every thought and action: in other words, it was memory – personal and collective memory.

I was filled with the knowledge that perception, thought and belief are often based on life experiences, indoctrination and human values. They are therefore transient. We think these transient masks are our only identities.

In that moment, in the Dome, I experienced a Light of Understanding.

I knew and understood that looking beneath, or indeed rising above, the personality formed by indoctrination, gender, creed, race and experience was the only way forward if peace was ever to evolve. Living and expressing ourselves through all these separate and conflicting roles created only fear, paranoia, pain and dis-ease.

Becoming consciously aware and 'light intentioned' is the mission of every incarnate soul on earth. Here, in this beautiful Dome, it all seemed so easy and possible. In this place, I truly realised just how amazing it is to be human.

Just as I thought these things, I became aware of Joshua and the crystal light giving such overwhelming love and value to every living soul on earth. I felt their compassion and their understanding of the tribulations inherent with living in this lower frequency, at the present level of consciousness on earth. The following message also came to me:

'You are light. You vibrate on many levels of frequency. Everything in the universe is light. Understand the science of light and you understand yourself and consciousness.'

The message continued: 'You are all from the light, but you have made the brave decision to join the cycle of birth and death. In this way, you live in this world of illusion in order to learn how to transcend it through experience and knowledge. You return to your parallel spirit world on your death where you train to come back again. Some of you stay in this realm to act as guides to those who return.

'There is now enough light for you to step into the New World, a very real world you have already created. Over aeons of time you have built this world with every thought and act of love, a very real world that exists parallel to your present world. It is waiting for you.'

Throughout time, many mystics have experienced the pure feeling of oneness. It is that feeling that I experienced myself the day I saw the Crystal Dome.

During this same period I had another beautiful vision that gave me new insight into The Work. I understood more about reincarnation and group souls and I watched in awe as the Soul Mothers sang to accompany a being of light down the continuum of light, in order to become part of the human race here on the earth plane. I understood what 'coming into our own' really meant when I saw each one of us as multidimensional beings, as sleeping giants, existing on a dimensional ladder of sound and colour, each one vibrating on a frequency of the light waiting for us to awaken them, to become them, to re-connect on the next step up the ladder. In a state of altered consciousness, as if watching a film, I was given a vision of a pregnant woman in the midst of a profound experience in which she was blessed with seeing her unborn child as he was birthed down the continuum of light to this material realm. This is what she saw . . .

The most indescribable feeling of love woke The Mother up in the middle of the night and tears fell down her cheek. How amazing to *know* her baby before it was born! She placed her hand on her stomach and sent her love and gratitude to the child who had been on its way to her for a very long time. "Let me be worthy of you" she prayed. He wasn't due to be born for another 33 weeks, but she had seen her beautiful fully-formed little boy. Just on the verge of falling asleep, in that state between the conscious and the unconscious mind, the mother entered a cave, a dark, warm, welcoming place where she was enveloped in the most gorgeous feelings of protective love. She dwelt for some time feeling wonderfully in harmony with heartbeat that sounded from deep within this cave. As her eyes adjusted, she became aware of a little creature that looked like a tiny tadpole encased in fluid. She had seen this image somewhere before, and then she realised, it was an embryo, it was *her* baby and she was in *her* own womb! As she glided towards her baby she stared in awe at this minute being. She could hardly believe that from this tiny alien swimming in this primeval pool of consciousness inside her womb would come a child who would run and laugh, cry and talk, who would think about the meaning of life, and who would love, feel joy, pain and loss and create life. As she thought of the miracle of life and the amazing gifts this child would give and receive she was shown a beautiful image of her baby's first smile that would bless her in the future. She looked and for the first time really perceived the sacredness of the birthing life-cycle. And as she did she saw another umbilical chord appear in front of her eyes, but unlike the other, this one was attached to the infant's head and was far more beautiful and radiant. She was drawn to the beautiful swirling mass of light and iridescent colour encapsulated inside this silver chord. Captivated and mesmerized she was magnetically drawn up outside her womb. Following this beautiful living chord she experienced pure delight, anticipation and excitement. But as she floated up higher she became more and more ethereal and peaceful. Entering this place of resounding light, she sensed rather than saw, the beautiful, serene, Mother Souls tending to the babies. They sang the most tender of ethereal, harmonious songs to each child who received and emitted the communion of pure, unconditional love.

This place was a replica of her womb but much more bright and beautiful, giving off an indescribable love she had never experienced before. For the mother it was like being present with God at a Divine Mass, and she too received the Maternal Blessing that entered her very being as these unseen light Mothers guided her to her un-born child. Although not due for a while there he was, this exquisitely, beautiful, fully-formed baby boy, cocooned and suspended in light. He looked into her eyes and they communed for an eternity. No words or thoughts passed between them, just the language of love. She saw the immense journey he had made to this hazardous world, towards of the great forgetting. He was now on the final stage before he entered the material world of illusion through her womb. She looked at this tiny, powerful being who could radiate enough light to fill the universe, but who had chosen to return, in diminished form, to this world. She realised how vast his sacrificial journey had been and it wrung her heart to think he had done this for her and humanity. He had travelled down the frequencies of light, and at each of the seven critical points of light he had remained there, suspended, bathed and cocooned, acclimatizing to this lower frequency before he continued on down.

Over eons of our time he had descended the ladder of frequencies, watched over by the Soul Mothers who would sing him down the continuum of light, sustaining him and birthing him time and time again into dimensions of diminished light. Their beautiful tones would create the most beautiful hues of colour from the pure white light, suspending, enveloping, and containing him in expressions of light until he could perceive a new and slower realm, before continuing his journey to Earth. At every stage he imploded his light, diminishing his radiating outwards in order to safely resonate in harmony with the lower stages of evolution. At each stage, as he moved down, he would leave his blue print, his encoded spirit D.N.A a blueprint, the map of light ready for his return. The nearer to the earth birthing he came, the more the light condensed and the one light became many colours. In equilibrium with him, the Soul Mothers' vibrational tones would lower and harmonise to express the limited rainbow colours we now perceive in the human world. The mother had heard of the 'music of the spheres'. She now saw how the human form came into being in the harmony of the spheres.

The lowered light and sound vibrations would enter the light-conceived spirit that would eventually be replicated in human form. The manifest brain would be the go-between, receiving and transmitting the limited light through the neural pathways, creating diverse and amazing expressions of life, as we experience it in our present limited state. Like the light, and in equilibrium, the brain was also perfectly limited in order to safely accept the amount of radiance needed in order to make sense and work out who and what we are. The abyss, the part of the brain not yet re-awakened was deep in meditation, waiting to be called upon to enlighten the journey home. These laws of light equilibrium are in parallel and operating throughout the universe. The measure of light expressed through the brain is perfectly synchronised with the measure of visible light and radiated light presently perceived in the universe. It is no accident that using just a small part of the brain, humanity perceives only a small part of the universe that the rest is presently perceived mainly as no-thingness.

The mother was made to understand that in the act of questing where we came we would be led back. After the birthing into this realm, a myriad of Soul

Mothers continue singing to the Spirits here on earth. They sing their sacred love and inspiration to children of light, helping to awaken them to their origins. They sing and they watch for our Spirits to awaken; when we shall be brought together in unison across the great divide, the void of the dark matter ready to emerge in a glorious explosion of light and sounds of a higher dimension.

Waiting for the wake up call, are our sleeping giants encoded with the spiritual D. N. A. of light. A light imprinted map has been left on, waiting to guide us back up in safety.

She opened her eyes and in gold letters above her was written.

D. N. A. OF THE SOUL

I AM

YOU CANNOT FAIL TO RETURN.

THIS IS THE SCIENCE OF LIGHT

ALL YOU HAVE TO DO IS

LET THERE BE LIGHT

AND THERE WAS LIGHT.

XXXXXXX

This was a powerful vision I was given help explain why we forget who we really are.

As we start seeking and searching, memory returns and we begin to realize that we are far, far more than our human selves.

My final vision was of Native American tribes – men, women and children in wonderful, vibrant, rainbow-coloured, feather headdresses that surrounded their bodies like wings. In my vision they descended from blue skies and returned to answer our call, the call to unify us, to consciously recreate heaven on earth.

I saw a beautiful blue sky and descending was a multitude of Spirits from all the tribes. They each had their own dress, embellished with beautiful beads and adornments, mainly of red and yellow, but the one thing they all had in common were their expansive rainbow wings that fluttered gently in the breeze as they descended to earth. One by one they came, men and women and finally the babies, cocooned in beautiful white buffalo skins, bringing the New Power to earth. As the rainbow-winged infants landed on earth, the white of their buffalo skins seeped into the red of the land creating a pink aura that quickly spread about and covered the earth.

These powerful beings grew in an instant to adult-hood. In the distance, the call of the eagle and the raven were heard. The Rainbow Peoples celebrated together in delight, and then slowly a profound silence descended and the people of all the nations joined together in a circle of dance. Two people from every nation, a man and a woman, each carrying a drum, formed an outer circle surrounding the united tribes. Then it started. Out of the silence, quietly at first, came one beat and another and then another and another until all the beats of every nation came together in a harmonic convergence of pure sound. As that one heartbeat of beauty reached the harmony of the spheres it changed the world forever in a twinkling of an eye.

Many humans have returned for many lifetimes, and each time they have increased their frequency a little. On every return each one has reconnected to the path they have trod before. Every reincarnated soul has left a footprint, a blueprint to walk again on their unique path of light vibration. Each soul has entities of love and light, helping and guiding them. We are never alone! We have a multitude of backing groups!

If people try to connect with these higher beings who are helping us together with their particular soul family with whom they resonate in love and harmony, then this will create even greater light. In these circumstances the law of spiritual synergy shall operate and multiply in light many more times the number of people communing with each other and in communion with the Christ-consciousness of our guides. This is above and beyond religion and dogma and is for everyone and every group to experience.

I received a message regarding beacons from the Spirit named Enoch in 2005: 'Awaken your sleeping giants and follow the signposts you have laid down over aeons of time to enlighten your return journey.'

In communion with the Spirit within I perceived a new light. I watched and listened for signs and was compelled to go places, on courses and pilgrimages, which always led me to people and experiences that made me release my old self and reveal another, much brighter me.

In August 2006, I visited my friend Aidan Story, a healer who works with angels, and from whom I had received help in letting go of patterns that were not helpful. He took me to the beautiful St. Teresa's Church in the centre of Dublin and the day after I was introduced to his friend Patricia Scanlan in the Usher Gardness. This was a huge turning point for me. I felt an immediate love that I had been led to these wonderful people.

It is not necessary to leave the house in order to join the inner pilgrimage and not everyone is able to travel as I have, but I have been fortunate to have visited places like Chartres Cathedral and the Gorton Monastery in Manchester and have been touched by their alchemical magic. I have been told to write to people on the directions of this Spirit and I have done so. I trusted totally this new shining path that had a magnetic quality and which directed me to do the things I would never have done if it had been left to my little ego claiming, 'You can't do that, who do you think you are?' Fortunately my spirit, which was coming into its own, knew the answer and didn't limit me. It was as if this new energy opened doors when 'little me' got out of the way and stopped obstructing the opening.

What I used to think of as 'coming into my own', I now term as my awakening. But it has taken over fifty years of experiencing the agony and the ecstasy of life, and maybe many lives, before I was ready to awaken. I now knew what I really was and had to do. When I asked the Spirit friends, years ago, how we would know when The Work was going to start, they would reply, 'When you come into your own you will know what to do without any one telling you – you will just know.'

I now know that The Work is in each one of us and is awakening to the light. I know we shall change the world in the twinkling of an eye. But how do we do this? In my meditations it has been impressed on me that I should meet with kindred spirits and enter 'the silence' together. The silence is where the divine resides within each one of us and is waiting for us to commune. Doing this in groups creates spiritual synergy and is exponential in its radiance and effects. This can be done anywhere but joining together in spiritually charged places is even better.

Your inner voice may tell you other ways to heal

and awaken but mine has led me to the following guiding principles and affirmations which I attempt to live by:

I am in service to the Light that knows and understands only love.

I speak only from my heart and spiritual mind.

I shall not make people feel any less than they are, for they are all of the Light.

Whatever I think, say or do to others, I do to myself.

I shall not waste my time highlighting the faults of others, they are only reflections of my own, but rather I shall look for their beauty, their love and their generous spirit.

I live in love, never fear.

I live in gratitude.

I should point out that most days I fail to live up to them, but I keep trying.

All we have to do is access the divine spark within. I surrendered to these powerful feelings – in fact it was irresistible. I seemed to be enveloped by a magnetic energy that not only compelled me to follow, but also led me to perceive with new eyes the miracle of life, the wonder of people and places. All manner of things were drawn to me, giving direction on my path of awakening.

Every time I moved forward on the path I was given another little gem, another piece of the jigsaw to follow. I was led by a series of synchronicities – unbelievable coincidences that seemed to have an intelligent relationship with my spiritual needs. A book would fall open at a page that would confirm the messages I was receiving or someone would ring and do the same. I would switch on the radio or television and there was an answer to a question I needed. It was as if the universe was an intelligent collaborator in my life. I am sure you have the same experiences all the time too and the more we are aware, the brighter and more frequent the signs become.

As well as these visions and messages I have since been led to places that have brought revelation and joy. It was in this way that the monastery in Gorton entered my life in 2008.

For the first time since becoming a mother I wasn't with my family on Mother's Day that year. My children were going away so we'd celebrated the day before. A spiritual friend, Eluna, told me about the monastery in Gorton – the place that we believe my great-great-grandfather, Martin Chaisty, would have helped to build in the 1860s, though I did not know that at the time. For around 120 years the monastery was a huge pres-

ence in Gorton but with the closure of the engineering works in the 1960s, the congregation
dwindled until the church finally closed for
worship in 1989 and the Franciscans left. It had
become derelict but was now being re-built by a
woman called Elaine. I got that tingling
feeling when Eluna told me the story and for a
few days I kept thinking about it. Apparently it
wasn't yet fully open to the public but you could
book to look around.

On Mother's Day I rang up to see if they had
an answerphone with information. Taken aback
when a man answered, I blabbed out that I had a
compelling feeling to visit the monastery. The man
explained that he wasn't usually there on a Sunday
morning, but he had paperwork to catch up on
because *Songs of Praise* had been televised there
the previous week and he had fallen behind. He
urged me to come straight away if that was my
feeling. I was so excited. I rang the friends I had
met and formed a deep connection with months
before, and we all rushed to meet at the monastery.
Eluna and I brought some candles and flowers for
our mothers in Spirit and of course for Mother
Mary and Mary Magdalene.

When we walked into this beautiful building
we were completely overcome by the feeling of
love. The six of us had a lovely little service by
the Lady Altar, a wonderful gift from Spirit. When
I got home I wrote up this moving experience and

was beaming for weeks after. It was so powerful that Simon and I volunteered to help and we have been there most Sundays since it opened to the public.

The excerpt from my diary was as follows:

On Mother's Day Sunday, 2 March 2008, I walked into Gorton Monastery and I knew this is where it would start. For sixty years I had held this time in my heart and in my prayers, and now here it was. The final manifestation of The Work would start here in this beautifully restored temple of light. A small band of lifelong soul-seekers and friends entered together and were changed forever. We were five: Simon, Harvey, Eluna, David and myself. We were greeted by a beautiful guide who had invited us immediately because we were compelled to visit. Tony, the guardian and historian of Gorton Monastery, led us through his inspired tour and 'the magnetic light' of the monastery did the rest. In this place, the Spirit of St Francis was repeating itself, but now 'his story' had become 'her story'.

In 1996 an ordinary woman with a successful career and comfortable lifestyle was about to embark upon an extraordinary and compelling mission to restore Gorton Monastery. Elaine Griffiths gave up conforming to all that was materially and emotionally safe and secure because she was to fulfill her soul intention. The only inten-

*tion the soul has when it returns to this realm is
to create more light in the world. Elaine and her
small team of family and friends have certainly
achieved that. They have not only restored a
building to its former glory and light intention,
but in so doing, they have created the environment where souls will awaken and be restored
again to their former glory. Sacred sites as well as
our souls have a blueprint, a DNA, that is enlightened when we come together in intention. Soul
synergy and this beautiful monastery shall create
alchemy together. In so doing, the multitude of
Spirits who guide and help to reveal our true
identity shall join us because we have consciously
joined them, and together we shall create light.
As the monastery becomes a beacon of light so
shall all the souls who enter.*

Tony invited Eluna and me to the monastery the
following week to meet the people who were
working there. Again, meeting the small band of
dedicated people – Elaine, Alison, Yvonne, Heather,
Kath and Karen – was a very powerful experience
and I immediate felt the link with my spiritual
kin. A few days later, whilst staying with Eluna,
who is a catalyst for me, I was compelled to write.
The following came:

> *Dear Elaine,*
> *It was lovely to meet you. Words cannot express*

the feelings of love and gratitude I feel for you. Walking into Gorton Monastery was like coming home. Your divine mission has created heaven on earth where a multitude of light souls can finally awaken.

The rebuilding of the monastery is spiritual alchemy of the highest order.

This is huge spiritual transformation that Spirit has worked to achieve for aeons.

Love and light, Pamela.

On 21 September 2008, on International Peace Day, a group of us joined together in the Monastery for an hours silence with people from all around the world. One day soon millions of us will do this in sacred places around the globe and Light shall increase exponentially. In the meantime we all need to prepare for this by 'Letting' the Light from within ourselves.

When I was young I was told very simply that I had two minds, the material and the spiritual. This I now understand. I can now see myself and the world at large from these two states of being at any given time. The material mind thinks it is separate from everything. It is full of humiliation, it fears differences and is defensive. The other mind resides in oneness and 'feels' from the heart in unconditional love.

There are three sayings that sum it up. The first is from an inspiring soul, Marianne Williamson, who awakened on 'The Course in Miracles'. Here she offers her wisdom on perceiving others:

'The places in our personality where we tend to deviate from love are not our faults, but our wounds. God doesn't want to punish us. And that is how he wishes to view the errors in other people: as their woundedness, not their guilt.'

The second is a wise Indian saying:

'A grandfather tells his grandchildren that there are two wolves fighting for the mind, one called Positive and one called Negative. "Who wins?" the children ask. "The one you feed," he replies.'

And finally another:

'Harbouring resentment is like taking a poison and hoping it will harm the other person.'

I recognise all those states in me and it is not easy to overcome, but becoming 'conscious of my consciousness' is a start. In this way my silent observer lets me see clearly where I am coming from and I can detach from the negative patterns that drive me and everyone else mad, and return to the mind of love and peace. Instead I dwell in the mantra that 'thought is a living thing' and I try to live in joy, gratitude and positivity in the knowledge that we are capable of amazing and miraculous things when we put our collective, powerful minds to it.

If we put our Spirit mind in the driving seat, instead of our material mind, we really could change the world in the twinkling of an eye.

The monastery also offered me wonderful

revelation of a more personal nature. Within a year of going there, I had a visit from an Irish relative, Siobhan, who had been researching the family tree. I couldn't believe it when I saw my great-grandfather living in Gorton as a boy. I had unknowingly followed in his footsteps at the monastery. It is no wonder I felt so connected.

It was at Gorton Monastery that I also learned of the connection between Manchester and Native American Indians. It is fitting, perhaps, to end by recounting one of Black Elk's childhood visions. The first one happened in the woods when he was five. It was thundering. Two men appeared on a cloud and he flew with them on his own cloud that came and lifted him up. These men came again when he was nine and was ill. He often heard them calling him, saying, 'Behold, a sacred voice is calling.' They took him to the centre of the earth where the six grandfathers reside in a rainbow tipi. Here Black Elk was given many gifts of Spirit. He saw himself as the sixth grandfather and he was given healing powers that would heal the world. He saw a sacred hoop and a flowering tree blossoming in the centre, which represented all the nations of the world coming together in peace. Black Elk was baptised a Catholic and helped to minister to his people but he was also a Lakota Sioux Holy Man. He wanted to share his vision as the sixth grandfather before he died.

I believe the flowering tree is taking seed in our

hearts and we are now ready for the message.

I would like to end with Corinthians 13, the reading Black Elk sent to his kind from Salford in 1888:

'If I speak in the tongues of men and of angels, but have not love, I am only a resounding gong or a clanging cymbal. If I have the gift of prophecy and can fathom all mysteries and all knowledge, and if I have a faith that can move mountains, but have not love, I am nothing. If I give all I possess to the poor and surrender my body to the flames but have not love, I gain nothing.'

Love is patient, love is kind. It does not envy, it does not boast, it is not proud. It is not rude, it is not self-seeking, it is not easily angered, it keeps no record of wrongs. Love does not delight in evil but rejoices with the truth. It always protects, always trusts, always hopes, always perseveres.

Love never fails. But where there are prophecies, they will cease; where there are tongues, they will be stilled; where there is knowledge, it will pass away. For we know in part and we prophesy in part, but when perfection comes, the imperfect disappears. When I was a child, I talked like a child, I thought like a child. I reasoned like a child. When I became a man. I put the childish ways behind me. Now we see but a poor reflection as in a mirror;

then we shall see face to face. Now I know in part; then I shall know fully, even as I am fully known.

And now these three remain: faith, hope and love. But the greatest of these is love.

Acknowledgements

I am truly blessed. This book of hope, faith and love has been inspired by so many from both sides of the veil. I owe so much to my ancestors and loved ones. Their pioneering spirit, their triumph over adversity, and their constant faith in The Holy Spirit has been the guiding light in writing this book.

Heartfelt thanks to the original circle of sitters for their dedication and for their wonderful and inspiring memories. Little did we know that their constant reminiscing was for a greater reason, and that sixty years later they would be shared in a book.

I live in love and gratitude to Jesus, to my Mam, and to the lovely spirit and angel guides for their unconditional love. Every morning I renew my prayer to be of service to The Work of Love and Light and to give thanks for being led on this wonderful adventure of Awakening.

Words cannot express the love and Gratitude I feel for the First Nation of Turtle Island, who in communion with The Great Spirit created the Sacred Land in which to welcome their brothers and sisters of all nations into the Sacred Hoop. I look forward to the future.

I hold a special place in my heart for Mother Mary and I am deeply grateful for her love and healing presence in Eire, at The Monastery, Manchester, at Chartres Cathedral, in Knock and Languedoc, and especially at Lourdes in June, 2010. Thank you to St. Bridget for coming to me and Trish in Dublin when we first worked on the book and for walking with us ever since.

Thank you Spirit friends for your constant reminders to 'Keep Faith in The Work' and for leading me to my Spirit family here on earth. So many have led me in love and healing to know myself. Through their example I have followed the Shining Path, watched for signs, listened to the inner voice, and followed in trust and delight.

The following Kindred Spirits have enlightened my path for which I am eternally grateful.

Two beacons of Light in Ireland, Aidan Story and Patricia Scanlan, whose lives and writings inspire us to 'come through adversity' and heal with love and forgiveness have been a huge influence on me and I am so grateful for their encouragement, support and loving friendship. Thank you both for your wonderful Irish hospitality and generosity of Spirit. Trish read and edited the first writing when it was just a stream of consciousness and she led me to Mark Booth.

My first encounter with Mark was under his nom de plume Jonathan Black when I read *The Secret History of the World* and I knew this timely revelation was special. In his book he describes Chartres Cathedral as an alchemical crucible for the transformation of humanity and I would go so far as to say that this book falls into this category too. Mark is also an astute publisher who has been quietly enlightening us with the many esoteric books he has championed over the past twenty years.

Thank you so much Mark and Charlotte from Coronet at Hodder and Stoughton and to Deborah and Lindsay for your dedication, support and amazing craft. Your friendship and patience has been unbelievable.

In June 2005 I was to meet wonderful new friends on Clive Koerner's Star Bourne workshop where I had my wake-up call to write. Sincere thanks to all the participants for creating the atmosphere where we could 'come into our own.' Thank you so much Ann for your healing, to Michael for showing me how to be fearless, and to Elaine for introducing me to Aidan. God bless you David for being a lovely companion on the path when it opened up five years ago.

Sincere thanks to my friend and philosopher, Mike Fuller. Your ideas and integrity has been an inspiration to me for twenty five years and I have lovely memories of our shared times with my mother who thought the world of you.

I am so indebted to The Rainbow Group past and present. I have learnt so much from you all, but most of all I remember the joy and recognition we felt when we first met. I shall never forget the love, the laughter and the inspiration I received from Ruth, Vera, Margaret, Helen, Derek, Sylvia, Clive, Freda, John, Paul, Ian, Dorothy, Pete, Jenny, David, Mike, Veronica, Joyce, Jean and John. There are many more, too many to mention, but you remain in my heart forever.

Much love to you Joyce for our healing walks and talks in Rivington. I treasure the years of meditation nights with you, Ken and our hosts, Edna and Burt who watch over us in Spirit. Thank you Trish Tidy for your expertise on the Cabala and for your joyful spirit.

A special thank you to Michael Stanley for your knowledge and love of Emmanuel Swedenborg and for the wonderful spiritual growth weekends in Purley Chase which I and my Mam loved. These are special memories.

The last five years has brought many new friends and insights into my life. I would like to thank Alison for showing me how to live an authentic life. I know you continue your work in Spirit helping prepare the new Souls returning at this special time. Thank you for our brief encounter and for your continued love and guidance Alison.

Love and thanks to my lovely friends Harvey, Pat, David, Maddy, John, Martha, Lubna, Paul and Julie for your friendship and support which has helped me to grow and to face changes with courage.

Thank you Eluna for bringing colour into my life and for your friendship, healing, and encouragement.

I am deeply indebted to you Harvey for your care, friendship and honesty in helping me to work on myself. Thank you so much Harvey for your hours of dedication to the Yantra, a wonderful, spiritual technique, which has helped me beyond words.

We are blessed with the team of Light workers who have dedicated their lives to re-building The Monastery in Gorton. To all the many kindred Spirits I have met at The Monastery I send sincere thanks for your lovely welcome and for our shared love of St. Francis and the Brothers whose love and light is imbued in every brick. I look forward to seeing Tony Hurley and Elaine Griffith's inspiring stories being published very soon. Love and thanks to Kath and Graham for your example and to Anne and Sue for your enthusiasm for *Hope Street* and for your delicious cakes!

Wishing Alison and Dawn at The Barefoot Foundation all the best in their inspirational work in leading the corporate world into a Spirited future.

Thank you Elizabeth for bringing your Labyrinth to The Monastery, it is a wonderful sacred walk.

Sincere thanks to the members, past and present, of Horwich Spiritualist Church for your service and your welcome.

Thank you to the Spiritualist movement for being a huge part in opening up this golden age of awakening. Andrew Jackson Davies, who pioneered the Spiritualist Lyceum, predicted this new dawn when in 1850 he said, 'When the Creeds and Dogma of the past have lost their influence and vitality, and man has attained a degree of development... and when his faith in the immortality of the soul has become almost annihilated by his struggles with his material nature... a new Revelation suited to his more spiritual needs should be vouchsafed.'

I have to mention how song and dance has been a constant blessing in my life. This year was no exception as I completed *Hope Street*. Thank you to the wonderful Horwich choir, Kadenza, for your welcome and your gift of African and freedom songs which took me back to my black and socialist roots. Thank you Theresa for introducing me to Alvin Ailey's American Dance Theatre which took my breath away and was indeed a religious experience!

Thank you so much Siobhan in Ireland for your family research, wonderful photographs and for introducing me to the ancestry sites that led me to Val in Australia and Diane here in Horwich. Thank you Bill for the documents and for your hospitality. Thank you all so much for your fascinating stories.

A huge thank you to the members of Horwich Heritage Centre, located at the Resource Centre, where I received so much help on the local and family history. Special thanks to Stuart, Sue, Betty, Geoff, Norman and Les for your time and expertise and to Geoff Pollit for your help and writings on the history of the telephone exchange, and to David Owen for your book and a captivating day listening to the history of your grandfather, the Rev. George Vale Owen.

One author who has written extensively on Horwich and Rivington is M. D. Smith and I highly recommend his books. In 1984 I bought his *Leverhulme's Rivington* which informed me of everything I know about Leverhulme and set me upon learning more about the amazing Lancashire Suffragette movement led by Emily Pankhurst. Thank you for putting me right David – as a child I really thought there had been an ancient Chinese civilization in Rivington!

Thank you Ataa for your inspiration, I can't wait to visit Damascus where I know I shall receive wonders untold. Thank you to Amanda and Tom for opening my heart through your healings.

To our lovely neighbours, Val, Gary and family who look out for us and support us in so many ways.

I have many friends too numerous to mention who have made this book possible. You know who you are and I am so grateful to have you in my life. Thank you to my work mates and the families who inspired me and who I shall never forget. Thank you Anne for your divine emails that always arrive when I need them. Thank you Helen and Mike for your friendship, your wonderful music and for the lovely nights of laughter.

To our lifelong friends, Gill, Col, Kate and Tom, I send deepest gratitude. We have walked together through the highs and lows of our lives and words cannot express our love for you. I know my Mam is never far away when we are together. Looking forward to our future dreams.

Thank you to Paul and Nila for our kinship and Native American bond, and especially for sharing your lovely girls Maia and Anu with us.

Love and thanks to you Auntie Alice for your constancy and for the laughter and the tears when we share the memories of our remarkable family.

To my loved ones who shared my Spiritualist childhood and their families, I thank you for your care throughout my life and for your wonderful memories that have beautifully coloured in this book of faith.

Finally, to my little family I send my deepest and heartfelt gratitude for your Love and the joy you bring to my life. I am truly blessed. Thank you Stephen, Joanne, Sandra and Ian for your encouragement and support for this book, but especially for making me a Grandma and letting me be such a big part in the lives of your gorgeous daughters. I am so proud of you all and I look forward to seeing Poppy, Sophie and Emma grow into lovely young women who shall change the world.

Simon, how do I thank you? It is impossible to say how much I love and appreciate you. You are a gift from God. Your patience and love is remarkable. Thank you for all the help on this book, for all the lovely meals and for your amazing comfort when I feel worried. But most of all I want to thank you for being a wonderful husband, father and a brilliant grandfather and for sharing wonderful times with me and the girls. I love you.

Let there be light

I have been asked to write an afterword for this paperback.

My personal afterword is 'LET'. To 'let' light has become my only mantra as we speed towards the changes that have been prophesied since time began. Whether we call it the end times, revelation, the golden age or disclosure, there is no doubt that we are making a huge transition into a new time when we shall reveal our true light.

We are seeing the collapse of forces that no longer serve the spiritual evolution and we are stepping into a new world that is becoming more and more visible. We are choosing love over fear and we are feeling this love. We are gathering and connecting like never before and the love is tangible.

Each one of us is a particle of the whole and as we shift in our personal perception we affect the collective consciousness – when the particle shall become the wave.

One month tomorrow from the date I write this – on the 11-11-11 – millions of people throughout the world will join together in silence for peace. This critical mass shall bring us into alignment with the divine plan in the twinkling of an eye and the world(s) shall change forever. We will integrate our light bodies on many dimensions and in communion with a multitude of light beings who have been called by the awakening of humanity. People will gather together in groups and in sacred places to commune and to give thanks that we are here on earth at this time of luminancy and celebration.

Here is a vision from the divine imagination that is now 'coming into its own':

'They experienced compassion, empathy and understanding of the Human Condition.

Instead of finding faults in each other, they now perceived everyone's gifts of light. They were all part of each other. They were each a facet of the whole. They were the Divine Plan. They had the same Mission. They were One. They were the Self-fulfilling Prophecy.

Finally, the Enigmatic John appeared in all his Radiance from the Spirit of the Violet Flame.

John The Baptist, had walked the Earth many times in many guises to prepare Humanity for the leap every time they were ready to take the next step upon the ladder of Light Frequencies.

Displaying the beautiful rainbow aura of their higher selves, humanity perceived the new world they had co-created.

This time they knew what they were and where

they were going. They were 'Light Intent'. The Wave of Light, observed in outer space but not understood by scientists, was drawing closer as if the Awakened ones had beckoned it. The Light that descended on Earth was both a particle and a wave as every enlightened Being became One with the Whole.

The Wave of Light vibrated as it swept the earth and LOVE became manifest throughout the Land. For the second time the Earth was flooded but this time the Baptism was not with water but with, INTENTIONED LIGHT.

The light formed a rainbow over the earth to reveal the second coming. The Messiah had returned and was the Christ consciousness of each and every Soul who had chosen to awaken.'